MARY PRATT

MARY PRATT

INTRODUCTION BY SANDRA GWYN

CRITICAL ESSAY BY GERTA MORAY

McGRAW-HILL RYERSON LIMITED

Toronto Montreal

CONTENTS

After encountering Mary Pratt's pictures, it's difficult to go back to thinking that baked apples and red currant jelly and cod fillets are ordinary. Or Saran Wrap, or aluminum foil, or a couple of eviscerated chickens perched, for the moment, on top of a Coca-Cola case, or even a bunch of brown paper bags bursting with groceries that tell of a hard morning's slog round the supermarket. Bold and flamboyant, but executed with the same kind of tiny sable brushes that Victorian ladies used for working their water-colours, her paintings have transformed these routine arte-facts of housewifery into aesthetic objects; the prosaic has become alluring. Because her work appeals to many people who aren't usually interested in art, she may have had more influence on shaping the way we see things than any Canadian painter since the Group of Seven transformed our perception of our bleak northern landscape. "The things that turn me on to painting are the things I really like," Mary says. "Seeing the groceries come in, for instance. Or cooking. I'm getting supper and suddenly I look at the roast in the oven or the cod fillet spread out on the foil, and I get this gut reaction. I think, 'that's gorgeous, that's absolutely wonderful, and I must save it.'"

This makes it sound easy. In fact, to all of these "gut reactions," seemingly arrived at by a kind of haphazard serendipity, Mary Pratt applies what she describes as "the sieve of my own experience," an allusive imagination that's as much literary as visual. Apples are an example. "When I'm painting them," she says, "the whole legend and mythology of apples occurs to me, and so Adam and Eve and the snake and all the rest of it somehow gets into the picture." She finds there's far more in fish than colour and texture and scales and bones. "They are symbolic of life itself, and of the sea. They are beautiful. They are the food, the sort of base food for us all, spiritually." There is always more in her paintings than meets the immediate eye. "I don't really paint beautiful things," she says. "There's always a little jog to the painting that makes it more complicated."

Two other qualities give Mary Pratt's paintings their special inner life. One is the presence of light. In the picture I know best — it's called *Bowl'd Banana,* and everything else in our living-room revolves around it — I never cease to be amazed at how a myriad of miniscule green and brown brushstrokes, almost invisible to the naked eye, suggest the sun shining through glass in a way that on a dark day is incandescent, like a votive candle, and that on fine days sparkles like diamonds.

The other quality is the palpable sensuality of her work, indeed, its eroticism. (That banana is a very *bold* banana.) For her, the act of painting may be an act of love. Sometimes, working alone in her studio, the intensity of creativity makes her weep. She has been described as the visual poet of the kitchen, but she is really a visual poet of *femaleness,* at once lyrical and tough-minded, and daring enough to deal not only with cosy female things like apples and fish and flowers and affection but also, as in for example the braggartly lascivious *Girl in Glitz,* and in the starkly sexual *Service Station,* with the darker, more complex emotions of pain and lust and anger and jealousy.

I first discovered Mary Pratt, not as an artist, but as a friend. When we first met — it was the summer of 1966, and we were both just over thirty — I had no idea that she was a painter. Like everyone else who turned up unannounced on the Pratt's doorstep, my husband and I had driven down to St. Mary's Bay, in the course of a flying visit to my native Newfoundland, in search of Christopher, whom I remembered vaguely from childhood birthday parties, and whose haunting study, *Woman at a Dresser,* had captured our imaginations in a recent exhibition at the National Gallery. As Mary remembers the scene, she came to the door and said the first thing that came into her head, which was, "Are you waiting to be welcomed?" My own recollection is more blurry. There seemed to be a lot of little kids sitting around a supper table. (As I later realized, there were four — John, Anne, Barby, and Ned — and that year, they were all under eight). There were also quite a few adults, for it was a Sunday afternoon, and Mary and Christopher were giving tea not only to his parents, but also to various aunts and uncles. We toured Christopher's studio and marvelled at how he was realizing his talent. What I do remember clearly is realizing instantly that Mary had been the inspiration for *Woman at a Dresser,* a chaste but sensuous seated figure looking in a mirror, even though her face was not visible in the picture. I also remember that then, as now, she had an expression that was at once merry and sceptical, and a laugh that was an outright guffaw. Perhaps — though this may only be hindsight — each of us saw in the other something of herself: we were both married to men on the brink of becoming important, and even as we rejoiced in this, we ourselves felt restive and unfulfilled.

Over the next couple of decades, as she started to paint and as I started to write ("Women from the Maritimes only start to grow up when they're well over thirty," I remember Mary remarking somewhere around 1973) we've managed to meet about every year, usually in Newfoundland, occasionally in Ottawa or Toronto. Time and again, I've been struck by her candour, by her pawky sense of humour, by the ability she shares with Christopher, not only to paint superbly, but also to be quite remarkably articulate about her work. Yet these occasions have usually been a bit frustrating because just when the conversation is really taking off, one or the other of us has had to rush off to get on a plane. It was only recently, after spending most of a week talking to Mary, in order to write this introduction, that I felt that after all these years, I'd begun to understand her.

◆   ◆   ◆

Except that it's also built of white clapboard, the house in which Mary and Christopher Pratt have lived for the last quarter-century doesn't at all resemble the square, austere, two-storey outport houses that so often appear in his pictures. Nor, for that matter — always a bit of a disappointment to visiting television crews — does their house look out on the sea. Rather, it's about half a mile inland from the head of St. Mary's Bay, a rambling bungalow on the banks of the Salmonier River, built originally in the 1920s as a "summer shack" for a St. John's "merchant prince." The Pratts have improved and modernized it beyond recognition. Yet the setting retains all its magic. Here, in the river valley, sur-rounded only a few miles distant by the quintessential Newfoundland landscape of boulder-strewn barrens, some quirk of topography has created a kind of micro-climate: rhododendrons bloom in the garden, as they do nowhere else on the island, and the lawns that sweep down to the river's edge suggest, reeds and all, a gentle English water-meadow.

Inside the house, the sense of being suspended inside an impressionist landscape continues. (Not long ago, when visiting Claude Monet's house on the Seine at Giverny, near Paris, I found myself thinking of Salmonier.) The living-room is big, white and airy, furnished comfortably but simply, and the wide windows frame the river, which doesn't flow past so much as it *glides* (often in two directions, because the tide reaches up this far). Beyond, on the opposite shore, rises a gentle hill of spruce.

When you move into the small dining-room, opening onto the neat modern kitchen — Mary prefers efficiency to nostalgia, and there is no attempt to create "the country-house effect" — the focus sharpens. Here, people who know her work always feel a shock of *déjà vu.* There, on the oval table, on top of a hand-crocheted cloth, sits the same Scandina-vian bowl that in *Three Gifts* holds grapes and apples and that in my own *Bowl'd Banana* contains not just the banana but also oranges and an apple. The table itself, without the cloth and bowl, and set with plain woven table-mats, blue-and-white knockabout china, and strewn with an assortment of ketchup and mustard jars, appears in the large glowing canvas that hangs on the Pratt's dining-room wall. This is titled *Supper Table,* and as we shall describe later on, it is one of the most significant pictures of her career.

The house speaks of serenity, and of a comforting sense of continuity. The children are all grown and married — there are already four grandchildren — but since they all flock down from St. John's on weekends, the light shining on the supper table often illuminates a crew that's as raucous and as ravenous as ever. As in their earliest years, Mary and Christopher share a 6:30 a.m. breakfast, then retire to their separate workplaces, meeting again for mid-morning coffee and for a hearty lunch that Mary prepares and serves promptly at noon. In the evenings, unless it's summer, and Christopher is out on Conception Bay racing his elegant sloop *Greyling* with his sons and his sons-in-law, they may read — Mary likes novels; Elizabeth Bowen and Margaret Drabble are particular favourites — or listen to music, or entertain friends, or simply keep on working.

Yet, over time, the change in the Pratt household has been subtle but sharp. In a sense, Mary doesn't live there any more. Her true habitat has become her studio.

◆   ◆   ◆

Mary's studio is an exuberant celebration of what she has so far achieved; it is also her own act of faith in the future. This is the work of art that she commissioned for herself in 1983, that she paid for out of the fruits of her own success, and that she planned down to the last detail. This is the "room of one's own" to which no one, not even Christopher, comes without invitation. When she goes to her studio, Mary treats it as an occasion to rise to. She never wears blue jeans, or paint-stained smocks. Indeed, it was only within the past year, when she began a new series of mixed media works that involve, in her description, "all kinds of messy new ingredients, like chalk and sprays and glue," that she regretfully abandoned custom-made shirts and skirts in bright colours and soft fabrics in favour of durable, washable, cotton-knits. It would be melodramatic to suggest that Mary Pratt, observed in her studio is a different woman than the one whom you will otherwise find. Any time, any place, the inner certitude without which she could never have become a painter at all, is almost palpable. What is true, however, is that within her studio, the slightly tentative, slightly self-deprecatory manner that Mary wears outside it dissolves. This isn't the tender and compliant young wife who inspired *Woman at a Dresser.* Nor is it the pretty, fifty-ish woman with marvellous clothes, an enviable complexion, and snapshots of grandchildren at the ready, who, if you spotted her across the floor at a crowded gathering, you could easily pigeon-hole as the "wife of" someone successful. As artist in her studio, within her own "cave of making," Mary Pratt is no one else's idea of her. Here, she has something in common with some of her own recent female figures, not the pouty and insinuating *Girl in Glitz,* but the assertive and electric *This is Donna.* Ultimately, in her studio, Mary Pratt looks exactly like who she is: a woman in the prime of her maturity and in easy command of her environment, a major Canadian painter at the peak of her powers.

Consider, more closely, Mary's studio. Physically, as much as psychically, this is far more than "a room of her own with a view." It's a small, self-contained house, built of white clapboard like the main house (to which Christopher's studio is adjacent), but standing about fifty yards distant, on a gentle rise on the opposite side of a noisy little brook spanned by a rustic bridge. There is a tidy foyer with flower-sprigged wallpaper, a deck out in front with pots of geraniums, a pretty little sun parlour with white lace curtains and white wicker furniture. (The chair is the same one upon which perched Mary's first female nude, *Girl in a Wicker Chair,* an enigmatic and sensuous painting that by its appearance on the cover of *Saturday Night* in September 1978, helped consolidate her national reputation.) The working area, roughly double the size of the Pratt's living-room, has a slightly different view of the river, but evokes the same feeling that you are inside a picture. As in the kitchen, all the working surfaces — tables, stools, desk, white mesh sliding storage baskets — are new and efficient. All is serene and orderly; yet despite the crisp modernity, this studio speaks of a sense of rootedness and of belonging. Unlike Christopher's studio, which is as pristine and geometric as one of his paintings, Mary's is pleasantly cluttered with what she describes as "women's stuff," a freight-laden phrase that will come up again later. There are jade plants. There are innumerable family photographs, some displayed formally in silver frames, others pinned casually to the wall. There is, curiously, a tiny model of an old-fashioned Singer sewing machine, and this will also come up again later.

Naturally enough, during the week that I was talking to Mary, we spent most of the time in her studio. Two things in particular shaped the direction of our conversation, for they seemed to relate directly to that immutable sense of self, which is her most striking characteristic. One was a small framed certificate hanging on the wall above her desk. It had a pretty art nouveau scroll around it, and it proclaimed that at Charlotte Street School in Fredericton, in the year 1942, Mary Frances West had got the highest marks in grade one. The other object was the painting that Mary was just beginning to work on. It was an interior landscape, a bit of a departure in her work, and it showed a staircase leading up to a second-floor hallway. "This is the house I grew up in," Mary explained. "This is going to be a picture about where I come from."

◆   ◆   ◆

That Fredericton house is built of sturdy, grey stone in the colonial style. The house is on Waterloo Row, and Mary's mother lives there still. Although the painting doesn't show it, there is also a river to look out on — the wide and placid St. John — but otherwise, the life that Mary led as a child has almost nothing in common with the life that became hers in Newfoundland. Unlike the Pratts, who were colourful and rambunctious and agnostic, the Wests were correct and controlled, and while not particularly religious, they went to church regularly, and did not question the established order. Everything in the house on Waterloo Row was done properly: the floors were polished to a high gloss, the bone china teacups and the carefully polished silver and the real linen napkins all had their proper places. People entered the house respectfully, for it revolved around Mary's father, William J. West, a Harvard-educated lawyer, who later became New Brunswick's Conservative attorney general and later still, a judge of the Queen's Bench. In the 1940s and 1950s, the temper of the Wests was reflected in the city itself. It was sun-dappled and stable. But it was also provincial and predictable.

If the Wests provided Mary and her sister Barbara, who was three years younger, with a childhood that even by Fredericton standards, was old-fashioned and prissy ("We weren't allowed to run all over town," Mary recalls. "We had to play in our own backyard.") they also provided them with, in her description, "a magic, idyllic world that was utterly safe and also utterly unique." In public, West was a crusty and rather scarifying individual, a strict teetotaller who once infuriated the other members of the Board of Regents at Mount Allison University by vetoing a brewer's proposal to build a hockey rink. In private, he was a lover of poetry, who read every night from Tennyson and Longfellow, and an imaginative storyteller who invented mythical characters in the tradition of *Alice's Adventures in Wonderland.* He was skilled with his hands, and built swings and teeter-totters and slides — even a proper playhouse with real French windows — that turned the backyard into a private adventure playground. Half a decade after West's death, he remains a dominant presence in Mary's life. "I thought Dad knew God," she reflects. "In fact, I was sure that he did."

The female influences in Mary's childhood were her mother, Katherine West and, more emphatically, her maternal grandmother, Edna McMurray. From Katherine, who was gentle and unassertive (she was nearly twenty years younger than her husband and had once been a stenographer in his office), Mary learned womanly things: the importance of running an orderly household, the importance of "keeping the peace." Grandmother Edna frequently created the need for peacekeeping. A large, generous woman of strong opinions, she had been known to vote Liberal, which made for pitched battles around the Sunday dinner-table. Within the context of the times, Edna McMurray was also a career woman: a detester of housework who had helped found the first IODE chapter in New Brunswick and served as its activist president for more than twenty years.

Mary was a round-faced, slightly plump little girl with short, curly hair. She adored pretty clothes, especially, as a photograph in the studio reveals, the gold slippers she wore as flower-girl at her cousin's wedding in 1940. She was also a bookworm, who loved *The Little Princess* and *What Katy Did* and (as she still does) *Anne of Green Gables.* "I remember," she laughs, "driving up the St. John Valley in the springtime, thinking it was so beautiful, and wishing I could do for New Brunswick what L. M. Montgomery had done for P.E.I." Early on, she began to look at things directly and wonder about them: why the bark on a birch tree was different from the bark on an elm; why the snowflakes had different shapes. She kept a scrapbook of clippings about Princess Elizabeth and Princess Margaret Rose (she's still something of a monarchist), but she also cut out the advertisements in *Good Housekeeping* and *Ladies Home Journal* that showed jars of yellow Aylmer peaches and quivering moulds of Jell-O. By the time she was seven, the Christmas her father gave her a little handmade desk with separate compartments for pens and Crayola crayons, it was clear that she had a real talent for drawing. A few years later, she got hold of some poster paints and produced a picture of a maple sugar bush that was selected for an international exhibition of children's art in Paris. "I used bright pink for the snow," she recalls with a guffaw. "When the other kids laughed, I made up a story that it was meant to suggest the idea of candy." Though her father told her not to get all puffed up ("They had to have something that looked *Canadian,* ") he quietly arranged for art lessons on Friday evenings.

In the autumn of 1953, at eighteen, she entered Mount Allison University, just down the road in Sackville, a place almost as unadventurous as Fredericton. But in those days, Mount Allison had the best fine arts department in the country; one member of the faculty was Alex Colville, then thirty-two. On the morning she registered, he asked whether she aspired to become a professional painter. "I hope so," she remembers replying, "but I'm terrified I might turn out to be just a Sunday painter." Colville must have spotted something in her manner and in her eyes. "You won't be," he said.

Her best year for studies was her first year. "Suddenly I started to learn in a formal way how to do things properly. How to get the shadows right, how to measure with your eye, how to make your hand aware of what the eye is doing." She was not William J. West's daughter for nothing; she took a decidedly dim view of fellow students who put on airs. "I just couldn't stand people who talked 'arty'," she remembers. "I didn't think they knew what they were talking about." Arty girls tried to look like Juliette Greco, arty guys aped Jack Kerouac, and when not proffering profound insights into Picasso and Jackson Pollock, they mocked New Brunswick provincialism. Mary defended it stoutly, and on one occasion this self-assurance about her opinions nerved her to take on the most glamorous figure in the Canadian art world of the 1950s, Alan Jarvis, director of the National Gallery, who'd come down to Sackville to lecture the students. "He told us how wonderful ugly art was," she recalls. "I jumped up and said, 'I haven't led an ugly life. Do I have to go out and find one in order to paint?' " Jarvis retorted, as Mary remembers it, "Oh well, if you want to join the Mummy-Bunny School." Today, she still takes an ornery pleasure in flying in the face of prevailing intellectual fashion, and when she addresses students, she frequently builds her lecture around a series of slides that celebrate and indeed even flaunt, her middle-class origins and conventional, family-oriented style of life. Unchanged by time is her bred in the bone conservatism, a conviction that present and future are part of a continuum defined by the past. Politically, she remains wholly William West's daughter, a Maritime Conservative with a Red Tory tinge, but make no mistake, a ferociously partisan one, much in the manner of Flora MacDonald.

No matter that she could sometimes be quite contrary, Mary and Mount Allison got on like a house on fire. She was a co-ed of the fifties in Black Watch kilts and Peter Pan collars, who enjoyed in roughly equal measure discovering Virginia Woolf and dancing the bunny-hop. Writer Harry Bruce was a fellow student and remembers her well. "She had dark curly hair, brown eyes, and an elegant little shape," he recalls. "She was bright, funny, and popular, and there was a powerfully appealing innocence about her." Bruce admired from a distance. He never got closer, because at the start of her second year, Mary West met Christopher Pratt.

◆   ◆   ◆

"He was standing by the window in the library waiting to register, and the light was shining right on him." There is still, after all these years, a thrill of excitement in Mary's voice. "He was wearing a bright blue sweater, and the bit of hair he did have was like a little halo around his head. I couldn't stop looking at him. I knew right away this was the good, and the true, and the beautiful."

As happens only in the movies, Christopher's reaction was identical. "The minute I saw her I had a premonition," he has said. "I felt there was something there." Theirs was not a classic 1950s white sports coat and pink carnation campus romance. Christopher was not a conventional suitor. He was not only the smartest person Mary had ever met, he was also the funniest. She recounts the time — both of us break-up midway through the story — that a professor set out to teach the Newfoundland students how to talk properly. His chosen instrument was the correct classification of pronouns. Down along the alphabetically arranged rows of students, the instructor moved solemnly. "Mr. Percy," he said, "what is 'you'?" Came the nervous answer, "I don't know, sir." The professor put the question to the next student. "Alright Mr. Pratt, what is 'you'?" Came the answer, deadpan, "I is a Newfoundlander."

Christopher was also moody and enigmatic, "a walking lump of young gloom," in Harry Bruce's neat phrase. "He was more demanding, in a masculine way, than anyone I'd ever known," Mary remembers. "He was an extraordinary combination of intense sensitivity and ferocious macho behaviour." The immediate problem was that Christopher had no idea of what he wanted to do with himself. He'd tried engineering and had given it up. Now he was trying out pre-med. Instead of dissecting frog's innards, he spent most of the fall of 1955 designing and painting decorations, on the theme of the popular musical *Brigadoon,* for the junior prom of which Mary was convenor. In his spare moments, Christopher was also painting water-colours that were more assured than any of the formal art students, including Mary.

Painting requires not only talent but drive, a hungry conviction that the talent must be expressed. Mary's contribution was to chivvy him and nag him and smother his self-doubts. Christopher today has not the least doubt that but for her he would have become a doctor, as his mother desperately wanted, or else a businessman, as all the Pratts (despite the maverick example of great-uncle E. J. Pratt) expected him to become. "It was she who gave me the determination to abandon all those other things and be a painter," he has said.

Christopher quit Mount Allison and went home to St. John's to paint. Mary stayed on and finished her fine arts certificate. They married in Fredericton, on September 12, 1957. "All the way down the aisle on Dad's arm," she remembers, "I thought, 'this is like Elizabeth Barrett eloping with Robert Browning. This is going to be something important.'" They spent their honeymoon on the high seas, aboard the little Furness-Warren steamer *Nova Scotia,* en route to Scotland, where Christopher had been accepted at the Glasgow School of Art. (As it happened, we crossed paths mid-Atlantic — I was aboard the sistership *Newfoundland,* coming home to get married, after a year in London.) Their first act on arrival was to splurge all their wedding present money on art books. That was the season when, give or take a few months, we were all twenty-two.

◆   ◆   ◆

A decade later, the Pratts had four children, and Christopher was well on his way to becoming famous. *Woman at a Dresser* had been shown at the National Gallery in a survey of recent Canadian work; *Time* magazine had reproduced his haunting serigraph, *The Lynx.* Many of the most influential figures in the art establishment — the dealers Dorothy Cameron and Mira Godard, and David Silcox, then head of visual arts at the Canada Council — had become his friends and patrons.

Meantime, Elizabeth Barrett Browning had turned into Mrs. Pratt. Visitors to Salmonier, including Richard and me, raved about her home-made bread and said the right things about her flower garden and her children. Nobody thought to ask about her paintings, because nobody knew there were any. "There was a terrible war going on inside my head," she remembers of this period. "I was furious that Christopher had somehow got it all together and that somehow I'd lost it."

She'd read *The Feminine Mystique* round about 1964, almost as if it were a samizdat journal. "It got me terribly upset," she recalls, "and yet I knew it was right." And yet not quite right for her. Unlike most of the women whose consciousness had been raised by Betty Friedan, Mary had never taken for granted that her role was to be a subordinate spouse. Rather — that first encounter with Alex Colville — she had been determined to have a career of her own. But she also wanted Christopher. Back at Mount Allison, she had convinced him that when it came to being a painter, it had to be all or nothing. "All" had turned out to be more than Mary had bargained for. Christopher's single-minded pursuit of excellence had not only swamped her own ego but had led her into a way of life that was utterly foreign to her. Knowing that this was every bit as much her own doing as his, and perhaps even more, simply fed her internal fury.

The first half-decade of married life had gone smoothly enough. Most of Mary's creativity went into having babies. In Glasgow, to her surprise, she'd felt fully at home. Even when pregnant, and shivering in a coldwater flat lit by a single naked light bulb, the gritty old city had beguiled her and she'd spent hours in its museums, marvelling at the way in which Rembrandt and Chardin handled light and shadow and texture. From there, they'd returned to cosy familiar Mount Allison for two years: Christopher qualified for his Bachelor of Fine Arts, and so did she, even though she now had two toddlers, John and Anne, to cope with. Later in St. John's, though the Pratt clan took a bit of getting used to, she was happy to settle down in a little suburban house and have another baby, Barby, while Christopher combined painting with running Memorial University's art gallery, and with both of them teaching extension classes.

In the winter of 1963, threatened by ulcers and an incipient nervous breakdown, and almost more by his students, whom he once described as "housewives booted out by their husbands on poker night," Christopher quit Memorial. Mary's moment of truth had arrived abruptly. Colville had just decided to leave Mount Allison. The university let Christopher know that the teaching job was his for the asking. Simultaneously, his father, J. K. Pratt, told Christopher that if he really wanted to be a painter full-time, the family's unwinterized summer cottage at Salmonier was available, rent-free. Mary, never told him outright, but as they both knew, she hoped he'd return to Sackville. Christopher chose Salmonier. The first morning they were there, he rose at dawn, saw a flock of eider ducks on the river, and took it as a sign of impending success.

"Those first years were so hard, it hurts me to think of them," Mary remembers almost with a shudder. The first winter there was no water in the house, and they had to lug it in from the brook. There were incessant power failures, and sometimes these lasted for a week. Soon she was pregnant again, this time with Ned. Winter and summer the in-laws were constantly descending, and while they brought voluptuous quantities of food, it was Mary who had to cook it.

There was a harsher problem at Salmonier. This was rural Newfoundland, the real Newfoundland, scarcely touched by Confederation. Just outside the pretty acre of the garden, with its rhododendrons, lay chaos. The austere, white clapboard houses of Christopher's pictures were metaphysical abstractions that had little to do with reality. The real Newfoundland was rusty, abandoned cars in front yards and beer bottles and Popsicle wrappers in ditches. Salmonier itself wasn't a picturesque community; even if it had been, its morale had been broken, like much of outport Newfoundland in that era, by welfare, by "resettlement," by the bureaucratic–industrial age crashing in upon a deeply conservative fishing society. On top of everything, Mary was a Protestant in a totally Catholic community, without Christopher's saving grace of being a Newfoundlander. "I felt like I was forgotten," she recalls. "I felt that I'd been cut off from my childhood and from everything I'd ever known."

Her response was to turn home and family into a cocoon that was also a citadel. Since she couldn't offer her children music and tennis lessons, she made up little poems for them about planting sunflowers and doing the washing in a rackety old machine with a wringer. She began a diary — which she still keeps — that was an emotional outlet. "I only have what is inside this house, this garden. I have to think everything is valid," runs one early entry. "I sit on the leather seat of a chair made by a man in Woodstock New Brunswick. I lean my elbows on a desk that used to be in my father's Carleton Street law office," she wrote with precision later. She seldom painted, but at every available moment, she drew the things around her: houseplants, the trees she could see from the window, little sketches of the children, or left-over pudding or egg-cups. "My only strength," she wrote in her diary, "is finding something where most people would find nothing."

For Christopher, Salmonier was working magnificently. By osmosis, from the river, from the air, from the sea, from deep within himself, but also from that overpowering Newfoundland sense of place from which his great-uncle had found the inspiration for epic poetry, he was finding his vision as a painter.

In a much more muted and nuanced way, Salmonier was also beginning to work for Mary. The Newfoundland way of being, raw, potent, slapstick, and tragic, began to interact with her own much more contained and repressed, but no less deeply ingrained Fredericton spirit of place. "I don't think I'd have been a painter at all if I hadn't come here," she reflects now. "This is an abrupt, dramatic, light-and-dark kind of society.

You're richer, you're poorer, you're wildly happy, or you're really depressed. The soft, romantic Goodridge Roberts approach that came naturally to me in the beginning doesn't apply here at all."

During these years, one of the few people in Newfoundland who knew Mary as other than Mrs. Pratt was the quirky, cranky, but exceptionally percipient South-African expatriate Peter Bell, who had succeeded Christopher as curator of Memorial's art gallery. He came often to Salmonier, and the spring of 1967, challenged her to put together a show. To the surprise of them both, she assembled forty-four individual works, ranging from a drawing of flowering broom done in Glasgow, to a full-sized oil of the garage at Salmonier, done the previous winter. The exhibition almost sold out. Her ego got a boost, even though she knew that her work was no better than competent, and just a bit polite and ladylike.

Mary's moment of illumination — it was that quite literally — happened the following year. She was mopping the floor in their bedroom when she got the first of what she came to call her "gut reactions." Suddenly, she found herself staring at the unmade bed and noticing it in a way she had never noticed it before. "The sheets were turned down and the sun was filling them with light. The red bedcover curled under the heavy, pink blanket, and seemed to drip onto the floor." All that morning, she painted frantically, trying to record what she had seen before the movement of the light altered the image. In the succeeding days, she began to notice other things — fish, fruit, bags of groceries — in this new and much more dramatic way. Her problem, she realized quickly, was that her moment of dramatic recognition was too fleeting. "The light wouldn't stand still long enough for me to catch it." (Nor could fish be left sitting on the kitchen counter until the same light came back the next day; indeed, in Newfoundland, whether the light would ever come back the same way was always doubtful.)

One evening, early in the autumn of 1969, when the westering sun began sifting through the dining-room window, Mary started getting prickles down her spine. "I asked Christopher to take the children for a while, because I just had to paint it." Christopher told her she was crazy. The light would be gone before she even got her paints out. She persisted, and started making a drawing. Christopher watched her, said nothing, left the room and came back with his camera. He took quick shots of the now fading light, shining onto the remnants of supper on the table. A month or so later he brought her the slides.

This was the true moment of illumination. "I could see so many things I hadn't seen before, all kinds of lights and shadows, and how a ketchup bottle hasn't just got an outside, but an inside too." She rushed to the spare bedroom she then used as a studio and, using the slide as a guide, worked in "an absolute frenzy of discovery." Even before

Supper Table was dry, she got another "gut reaction" to a mess of freshly caught herring laid out on an empty, fifty-pound salt bag made of polyethylene, which she photographed and again using the slide, painted another picture, and then another of baked apples. These works were utterly unlike anything she had done before. There was nothing tentative or ladylike about them. They were bold, frontal images full of energy and attack. The first time I saw them, dropping in at the Pratts on a rainy autumn evening, I was astonished. I remember thinking that it was as if Andy Warhol had suddenly started painting like Chardin.

Supper Table marks the real start of Mary Pratt's career. "The camera was my instrument of liberation," she says. "Now that I no longer had to paint on the run, I could pay each gut reaction its proper homage. I could paint anything that appealed to me: Barby eating an ice-cream cone, a dish of trifle in the garden, whatever. It also meant that I didn't have to fuss all the time about the drawing. I could use the slide to establish the drawing, and concentrate on the light, and the content, and the symbolism."

Mary being Mary, she nevertheless soon began to ask herself disquieting questions. Was she being dishonest? Was the sheer fun and ease of the new technique tugging her towards the slick and the meretricious? Peter Bell pursed his lips and tut-tutted. Her parents, William and Katherine West, were distressed at what seemed to them a loss of integrity. Some friends asked why, if she wanted a picture of something as humdrum as herring on a salt bag, she didn't just take a snapshot of it.

In December 1970, right in the middle of what was to be her most ambitious work so far, *Eviscerated Chickens,* Mary dismantled her easel and put away her paints. She decided to take up sewing instead. It wasn't a joke — she actually signed up for a course of lessons — but the family decided to treat it as such. At Christmas, the children clubbed together and gave her scissors, thimbles, and the miniature Singer that she now keeps in her studio. Christopher gave her a small, neatly beribboned package that contained two slides of the chickens and the message. "Please finish this picture, because if you don't, I foresee a long future of taking flowers to the mental hospital on Sunday afternoons." In the silence that followed the opening of the presents, seven-year-old Barby piped up: "Mummy, if you're not a painter, what can you be?"

A few days later, she returned to her studio. Christopher's wit had led her to the truth. So no less, had Barby's question. "I thought, Oh my God, I can't let the girls down. They can't see me falter now. What will they do when they themselves grow up?" As for using slides, Mary discovered that they worked for her, that the works they produced justified themselves and that, "not to hide behind a lie," she would explain what she was doing, even before anyone asked. The decision was her own, but later she found plenty of intellectual legitimacy for her technique. Not only had Degas used photography as a tool for establishing the precise movements of the racehorses he so often painted, the camera itself was the direct descendant of the camera obscura that Vermeer had employed in pursuit of his own responses to light and shadow.

◆   ◆   ◆

Early in 1971, Mary's paintings were seen for the first time outside Atlantic Canada, when the Picture Loan Gallery in Toronto featured several in an exhibition of Newfoundland art. *The Globe and Mail* reproduced one, and in its cutline, described her work as "a fresh whiff of the sea from St. Mary's Bay." (Dorothy Cameron sent her the clipping, with the note: "Who's the artist in this family, anyway?") In 1973, Erindale College gave her a Toronto show of her own, and the following year, Edythe Goodridge, who'd succeeded Peter Bell as curator of Memorial's art gallery (and later became head of visual arts at the Canada Council) assembled a partial retrospective that moved on from there to Simon Fraser University in British Columbia. The big breakthrough came in the autumn of 1975, when a dozen of her paintings, and several of her drawings, were shown at the National Gallery, in a major exhibition curated by Mayo Graham, "Some Canadian Women Artists." All of a sudden, all the things that had happened for Christopher a decade earlier, were happening for Mary. Her work was powerful and original. Above all, it was accessible. People were delighted to see onions simmering in a Pyrex saucepan and jars of red currant jelly that they almost expected to feel sticky to the touch. Realism was back in favour. Critics compared her to the new breed of New York photo-realists, like Richard Estes and Chuck Close.

A more consequential piece of luck for Mary was that her appearance on the scene was cued to the rise of the women's movement. Well before the National Gallery exhibition, itself a by-product of International Women's Year, reproductions of her work had started turning up in study kits assembled for the new women's programs going into place in universities and high schools. Feminists embraced her as one of their own and lamented that her artistic flowering had been so long delayed. Much was made of the fact that just before leaving Mount Allison, a professor had drawn her aside, told her that there was room for only one painter in a family, and that obviously, this was going to be Christopher.

Mary herself has always been ambivalent about being constructed into a feminist heroine. "I think of myself quite consciously as a woman painter and I have quite strong feelings about the women's movement, without being really part of it," she remarked in 1975. "I sometimes worry that because the things I paint are women's things, people will assume I'm trying to get ahead by using the movement. I have a lot to thank it for, but not for the origin of the work, not the impetus to paint. I do think that it's important for a woman to work within her own frame of reference, and not feel it is inferior to feel the way a woman feels. The minute you try to adopt the mannerisms and attitudes of men, it all breaks down." In short, while wholly female, and celebratory about it, she is at once too conservative and too independent-minded to be, as she puts it, "coerced into a sisterhood."

As Mary emerged into the public domain, she enjoyed a further piece of luck. Though apparently shy and unworldly, she turned out to have a remarkably canny knack for publicity. Her candid quotes and well-told anecdotes delighted magazine writers — from *Saturday Night, City Woman, The Canadian, Maclean's* — dispatched by editors anxious to fill up their regional quotas. She was the perfect success story for the seventies, a "wife-of" turned into a star, a warm, witty, "Whole Earth Catalogue" kind of lady, who had a storybook house and storybook children, who was a dab hand not only at painting wonderful pictures, but also at baking wonderful bread.

Unlike many other media creations of that era, Mary had staying power. A decade later, in the hard-edged, late eighties, she had become a major figure in the Canadian art world. Her works fetched five figures. Her dealer was Christopher's dealer, the demanding and discriminating Mira Godard. She'd had major retrospectives at both the London (Ontario) Regional Art Gallery (1981) and the McLaughlin Gallery in Oshawa (1983), and from the middle of the decade, important bi-annual shows both in Toronto and at the Equinox Gallery in Vancouver. Her image of a mackerel had flown high on a billboard over Toronto. From Kelowna to Cornerbrook, she was in demand on the lecture circuit. She had her own illustrated entry in *The Canadian Encyclopedia.* She'd become a public figure: Memorial, Dalhousie, and St. Thomas University all granted her honorary degrees. In 1982, she was appointed a member of the Applebaum-Hebert Committee, established to inquire into the state of the arts in Canada; in 1988, she was appointed to the board of the Canada Council. (She herself has never applied for a grant.) When doing her "public duty," as she describes it, Mary is a bit uneasy. "I don't know anything about bureaucracy," she says, "and because my own life has been so isolated and idiosyncratic, I don't even know all that much about other artists' needs." But as Bill West's daughter, she couldn't deny the responsibility to give something back. "Maybe sometimes I manage to ask the right foolish questions," she reflects. "Maybe sometimes I get the point across that the arts are bigger than either the arts bureaucracy, or the organized arts community, that somehow, we have to find some way of making them part of the larger society."

◆   ◆   ◆

"Where I was born and where and how I have lived is unimportant. It is what I have done with where I have been that should be of interest." The author of this comment is clearly not Mary Frances West Pratt, whose work has been so clearly a visual diary of the minutiae of her existence. It is instead, the late American painter, Georgia O'Keeffe, with whom Mary has in common a streak of orneriness, an adamant sense of self, and as demonstrated in some of her own drawings of flowers, executed in the mid-seventies, and partially inspired by O'Keeffe's, the same ability to convey not so much surface beauty as the arrogant life-force within.

It is when you confront the dozen or so paintings within Mary Pratt's body of work that stand quite apart from her mainstream, that O'Keeffe's remark becomes point of entry. Consider, as the most dramatic example, the dead moose in *Service Station* (1977). This harrowing image of female crucifixion and rape has something in common with O'Keeffe's celebrated painting *Cow's Skull: Red, White and Blue* in the Metropolitan Museum, something also in common with Rembrandt's *Flayed Ox,* that Mary long ago, must surely have lingered over in Glasgow's public art gallery. Here, for reasons that she can't entirely explain, except to say that this too was a "gut reaction" of a quite different order, Mary has transformed a commonplace incident of her life in rural Newfoundland ("Hey," the man at the local garage had said, "want to take a look at my annual moose?") into a universal image of violence and acquiesence. The direct reverse of this image, equally startling, and at once inspiring awe and celebratory, is to be found in the painting of 1983 called *Child with Two Adults.* Here, the ingredients of a sweet, tender, feminine set-piece in the tradition of Mary Cassatt — the subject is Mary's first grandchild Katherine, being given her first bath — becomes instead a powerful and declamatory affirmation of life, in which "the child, red-raw and slippery-wet is a tight knot, a closed bud, a blood-coloured bundle of fierce potentiality," as the critic Nancy-Lu Patterson has remarked.

Mary describes these darker pictures as works of "social comment." Few in number, they may be her most important works, and the ones for which she will be best remembered. Critics puzzle over these visceral and often disturbing statements about the human condition, in particular about the female condition. Yet even as they admire, critics express regret about what they construe as a lack of coherence in her work, a tendency to advance an idea, seemingly out of the blue, but not to pursue it through other images, an unwillingness to push through difficult concepts to a conclusion.

An obvious reason that these works appear infrequently is that they're gut-wrenching. When Mary is working in this vein, the brush seems an extension of her nerve ends. Consider the erotic series of female nudes that begins with *Girl in a Wicker Chair* (1978) and culminates so far, at any rate, with *Donna* (1986), *This is Donna* (1987), and *Girl in Glitz* (1987). "I'm painting a woman looking at my husband," she explains. A woman who is looking at him speculatively, that is to say. In these paintings, Mary Pratt, in her own words, "is coming as close as I ever care to come to making statements about my own situation."

We cut now, very close to the bone. We are intruding upon intimate territory. Once, as in *Woman at a Dresser,* a painting that a distinguished British critic likened to Vermeer, Mary was Christopher's inspiration, and sometimes, as in *Woman at a Stove,* his actual model. She was always his muse. Her body, soul, and intellect served his art. Then — child-bearing among many other considerations — he began to employ local Salmonier girls as models. He's an exceptionally attractive man. This is only the first and the conventional layer of tension. The relationship between Christopher and Mary had been quite uncommonly, indeed uniquely intimate. They lived in isolation. They talked, discussed, argued, in passionate and articulate detail about painting — about *his* painting. John Donne's twin compasses, moving in perfect union, was the verbal correlative of an almost metaphysical relationship. Then she too became a painter, an important one, with her own need for space, her own demand for attention.

Mary and I can talk about this because some of our experiences are similar; even more because she is so extraordinarily candid. When she decided to paint the female figure, she chose deliberately to use the slides Christopher had taken of his models. She treated them as "found objects." "It's not what you see," she remarks, "it's what you find." Often, to Christopher's disquietude, she has found far more than he realized was there. "I wouldn't use the term 'voyeur'," he reflected to me, "because that does not describe Mary's reaction. But she was looking at a naked woman who was looking at me, she was a spectator after the fact at a very private circumstance, and there is all the literary dimension about the precedents and the antecedents of the particular moment shown in the photograph." To her own disquietude, Mary has also uncovered primal emotions within herself. *Girl in My Dressing Gown,* for instance, speaks unmistakably of archetypal female rivalry no matter that the model in question, Donna Meaney, was and still is a good friend of both of them. In the case of *Girl in Glitz,* the model was a stranger, and Mary's discussion of her own feelings is detached and even clinical. "There's a tentativeness in her eyes, she doesn't know whether to be sexually interested or not. It's a wonderful, lush image, but on her stomach, there's the mark of a buttonhole from her jeans."

It is only because the union between Mary and Christopher is at once so strong and so tensile that an outsider can enter upon this intimate territory. And there is an objective, non-voyeuristic reason for entering. Their ferocious candour about their feelings, their unflinching self-analysis, informs and gives strength to their work. Time and again, while researching this piece, and indeed, for as long as I've known them, I've been struck by the fact that for both partners, that first principle of Socrates, "The life which is unexamined is not worth living," is their own first principle. Independently, and together, they have arrived at a central truth, one that the American novelist Alison Lurie has expressed in her comment, "If nothing will finally survive of life besides what artists report of it, we have no right to report what we know to be lies." Their life together has never been easy, not at all the gingerbread idyll portrayed in so many magazine pieces. Mary's success has made it incomparably more complicated. All marriages in which both partners are trying to fulfil themselves creatively take effort to sustain; when both partners are trying to be creative in the same area, the effort is all the greater. Some people — Richard and me as an example — work it out by cultivating a kind of symbiosis, a mutual "feeding upon each other," in which each other's creative and technical difficulties are talked out obsessively.

The Pratts, in the years of their maturity, have cultivated a gentle apartheid. Indeed, they do not particularly like being known as "The Pratts," and Mary nowadays rather regrets that at the time of her marriage she rejected her mother's advice to use her maiden name professionally. Despite their close physical proximity, they rarely visit each other's studios and although, over the supper table, their talk frequently centres around their work, this usually involves the small change of schedules and logistics. ("On questions of technique," says Christopher, "Mary is the painter around here. She has a true classical understanding of how to mix paint and put it on canvas.") Yet about what really matters, they remain indivisible. No critic has ever been more eloquent and incisive about Mary's work than Christopher. In a private diary entry describing her 1983 retrospective that he showed me, he wrote, "It is technically and physically substantial, concise, condense, contained. It is intellectually honest, apparent without being superficial, literate without being narrative, articulate without being glib. Her paintings are incalculable enrichments of the slides from which they proceed, and that enrichment is both visual and spiritual."

As for Mary, second only to becoming a painter, she counts as her finest achievement the fact that all those years ago at Mount Allison, she made Christopher recognize his destiny. "As an artist," she says, "I'm not really at his level. My intellect isn't powerful enough, nor profound enough for me to be there." This isn't false modesty, still less has it to do with male–female or husband–wife relationships. Rather, it's the recognition of the fine, uncharted line that separates genius from talent of the highest order.

All of which becomes impossibly solemn when you actually observe Christopher and Mary kidding around with each other: he hamming it up like a character from CODCO, she playing both audience and straightman. What you realize swiftly is that there's another critical factor involved in this marriage, and it may be the most important one. Laughter is the best tension solvent of all. If Christopher, thirty-five years into this partnership, keeps on being the smartest person Mary has ever met, he also keeps on being the funniest.

◆   ◆   ◆

"If women are the muse for men," Mary reflects, "what is the muse for women?" We had reached the point when conversation was turning to the future. Nowadays, as Mary approaches her mid-fifties, the 'gut reactions' no longer arrive in such splendid profusion, and she is becoming increasingly concerned with developing a philosophic frame of reference for her painting. "Time and again, I ask myself, 'What is this all about? What is it, inside me, that makes me want to create?'"

She has been reading, more voraciously and eclectically than ever before. The Bible. Santayana. Literary biographies of other creative women like Vita Sackville West and the British painter Gwen John. The journals of L. M. Montgomery. Yet for Mary Pratt, the truest and most original answer has emerged, as always, out of the fabric of her own life.

"Women's stuff" is the phrase she has coined to define this female muse. She means by this the energy that accrues to women out of small things around them: the food that has to be cooked, the socks that have to be picked up, the thank-you letters that have to be written. "You pick up an inkpot," she elaborates. "You know that that comes from Germany; you put it beside a lamp that comes from California; you put it on a table that is made down the street. You pick up a jug that someone gave you for a wedding present, and it's almost like saying hello to that person. You are aware of all these things, you know when your children's birthdays are. You know all these things because this is the stuff of life, that stuff that everyone touches everyday, the stuff that a woman understands."

Mary's point of view is at once old-fashioned and post-feminist. It's an expansion of the comment she made long ago in her diary, "My only strength is finding something where most people would find nothing," and an expansion also of her conviction that women can only fulfil themselves creatively by working within their own frame of reference. "Women are different from men," she emphasizes. "Their special role is to convey to men their own reverence for the small and the seemingly unimportant. It's almost like the apple that Eve gave to Adam. This is what I give to you, this is what I have, this is what I understand and you don't."

For Mary, "women's stuff" is inseparable from her deep and protective — sometimes perhaps almost over-protective — maternal instinct. It's significant that her own favourite among her paintings is *Child with Two Adults.* If, within the marriage, Christopher has played the dominant role, neither would disagree that within the family, Mary has been the organizing principle. To each of her four children, she has always been exceptionally close, at once the disciplinarian within the household — when they were little, she outlawed the phrase "It's not fair" from the household vocabulary — and a best friend and confidant. "Mom's studio was always open to us," recalls her younger daughter Barby. "I'd go there often to do my homework, while she was painting, and if I asked what she was doing, she'd explain why she liked to paint tin foil and Saran Wrap and why these things were important to her. I remember when I was about twelve, she was painting the moose in *Service Station.* I thought it was horrible, but when she began to explain it, I began to understand."

Given their genetic heritage, and the environment in which they grew up, it isn't surprising that all four Pratt children could have become artists. Indeed, Mary keeps in her studio a remarkably accomplished landscape painted by her elder daughter Anne, when she was in her teens. But in the event, both Anne and her elder brother John have chosen to channel their talent in other directions, she as a freelance reviewer and advertising executive, he as a scientist turned lawyer, with a particular interest in environmental issues. It is the two younger children who have set out on a life in the studio: Ned, a recent graduate of the Nova Scotia College of Art is a highly promising photographer; Barby (who asked long ago, "Mummy, if you're not a painter, what can you be?") is at the start of her own painting career, as Barbara Pratt Wangersky.

Among the children, it is Barby who most resembles Mary. The likeness isn't physical — Barby is fair-haired and blue-eyed, like Christopher — so much as spiritual. There is the same independence of mind and single-mindedness of purpose; talking to Barby, it is easy to catch an echo of the fifties college girl who dared take on Alan Jarvis. There is, more particularly, the same deeply feminine impulse to paint from a "gut reaction." If it was bold, twenty years ago to celebrate tin foil and Saran Wrap, it is bolder still, as Barby is currently doing, to transform ephemeral, chopped up illustrations from fashion magazines into vivid and sensuous paintings. "It was Mom who gave me the confidence to plunge ahead and do what I really wanted to do," Barby told me. "She always said, you have to paint what you like, and what you enjoy looking at. In the back of my head, I hear her saying, in her studio, 'Isn't that wonderful? Don't you just love it?' I'm not laying it on. This has become almost a religion for me."

Mary herself isn't yet sure where her own new understanding of female creativity will take her. One signpost is her recent thematic exhibition "Aspects of a Ceremony" in which she used the apotheosis of "women's stuff" — the weddings within a month of each other of both Barby and Anne — to create a visual, allegorical essay on the ceremony of marriage. Another is the pre-Raphaelite portrait, *Venus from a Northern Pond,* that was the centrepiece of her major 1987 exhibition in Toronto, and in which she attempted to give visual form to the female muse. She is thinking of making a film, or perhaps even doing an installation piece, though the idea of creating a work accessible only to an initiated minority goes against her grain. For the first time, she has begun to use mixed media — water-colours, pastels, gouache — in a new series of much looser and larger-scale work than she has previously attempted.

Whatever the case, while this biographical profile and Gerta Moray's critical essay documents Mary Pratt's life and work up to now, this will not be the last word on her. She will keep on being the woman for whom each moment in the studio is an occasion of celebration. She will keep on surprising us.

Sandra Gwyn

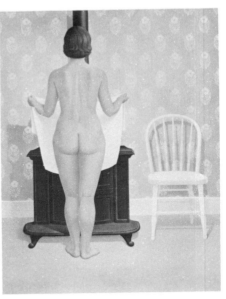

Mary Pratt's pictures are paintings done after the death of painting. The invention of photography in the nineteenth century robbed painting of its monopoly of the visual record. "From today painting is dead," French artist Paul Delaroche declared, when he saw his first Daguerrotype in 1839. This "death of painting" has haunted art ever since. Rebelling against its newly enforced subjectivity, painting tried to devote itself to logic, to universality, and found itself, through the pursuit of abstract qualities, reduced to its ultimate conclusion: the monochrome canvas. Hence, Russian Malevich's white on white, and American Ad Reinhardt or Canadian Ron Martin's black on black. Retaining its status of luxury object, painting lost its role of creating the contemporary image to the modes of mechanical reproduction. So today new media dominate our culture, not only in the commercial arts, but in the work of many "fine artists" who use photography, video, or film.

The strength of Mary Pratt's paintings lies in the fact that they admit this situation. They openly acknowledge the photograph, which is inseparable from the process of their making. They acknowledge a relationship to commercial art, through their close-up and seductive presentation of objects. They acknowledge their relation to painting in the past, but also their difference. The old *genres* are here: still life, the female nude, occasional views of an interior or of a landscape (usually seen from, or around, a house). But in the face of painting's historic claim to an elevated ideal, Mary Pratt presents us with everyday objects caught at a particular time and place by the camera.

At first sight, Mary Pratt's paintings seem like the most natural and direct reflection of her environment, but they depend on a complex process of picture making. She confronts us, in fact, with paintings of photographs of objects. And these have become images that implicate, in their look and in their making, a number of visual codes: photography, advertising, painting, the conventions that define social constructs. Each is a code that implies a particular and different relationship to reality. Their co-existence in Pratt's paintings sets up tensions and highly contemporary nuances of meaning.

This book, in turn, presents photographs of these paintings of photographs, and three texts, each of which aims to restore the presence of the paintings through a particular frame of reference. There are the artist's own words, recalling for us the circumstances in which the image was found, the associations it has for her, technical details of its execution. Then there is an appreciation and biographical profile by a friend who is a writer. The point of view of *this* text will be that of an art historian, intent on placing Mary Pratt's work in the wider context of art in the latter half of the twentieth century. It will point to meanings and resonances that are suggested when her work is looked at as an intervention in the artistic debates and issues of the period.

For Mary Pratt has found her own voice in a language that is open to the multiple codes of both past and contemporary media. A particular regional environment, such as the Maritimes, may retain more links to the past than the city does, but it is not immune to the pervasive influences of technology and mass media. Mary Pratt was never fully satisfied with the given artistic conventions at her disposal. She found them affected and "arty," inappropriate to her vision. I shall consider, in turn, the different layers of meaning set up in her paintings through their relationship to photography, to painting, to religious imagery, to advertising, and to femininity as it is constructed in our society.

◆

"Every photograph is a certificate of presence."
"All those young photographers who are at work in the world, determined upon the capture of actuality, do not know that they are the agents of Death."
ROLAND BARTHES (1981)

Mary Pratt established her distinctive style as a painter when she adopted the photograph as a tool. Why did this make the distinctive difference? As she has said herself, the photograph made it possible for her to capture particularly intense moments of vision, moments that were by nature unpredictable, fleeting, and often characterized by momentary qualities of light which gave to them a particular sense of revelation. These intense moments of vision were subjects she had tried in vain to paint directly from the motif. The processes of painting were not swift enough to record the transitory qualities of the visual scene which had triggered in Pratt a strong emotional response that prompted her to paint. If she had a photograph of that scene, she then had a permanent record from which she could re-create the magical moment of vision. Thus began her involvement with the camera image.

The camera is a mechanical apparatus, but the photograph that it produces is more than the product of a machine. It bears a unique relation to its subject that has important implications for the human viewer of that image. In the photographic process, reality itself imprints its own image, through reflecting light from its surfaces onto the photosensitive film. The photograph is therefore usually a direct trace, a deposit, an irrefutable testimony that something was there at a particular moment. But this image, so magically preserved, is also by implication a symbol of loss. For what is recorded there is tied to the moment in time when the record was made, and so, by definition, is irretrievably past, dead. This is what gives photographs their poignancy.[1]

Mary Pratt's paintings incorporate this certainty of the photograph, while seeming initially to repress the dimension of loss. (Of this, more in a moment.) Her paintings tell us they are a clear and direct record. Her accounts of how she works show that she proceeds as much as possible like the camera itself. This is not the abstracting of schematic relationships within the visual field that make the traditional painter's work, from drawing or sketch to painting, an independent creation parallel to nature. It is, rather, a submission to the standards of veracity of the camera and to its limitations. Like many painters of her generation, Pratt works from the assumption that to see with the camera is a natural mode of vision for contemporary viewers, to be accepted as a norm.

The photographic image has visual properties which are interesting in themselves (different depths of focus, blurring, over- or under-exposure, and contrasts of lighting) that Pratt has increasingly explored in her paintings in the eighties. From the outset her process of working from the photograph has been open to the experiences of scrutinizing the photograph. She has described her delight in finding that there is an abundance of visual detail to be discovered in the photographic image — details that the eye had not registered in the moment of discovering the scene itself. The painting done from the photograph is, then, a record of a meticulous scrutiny of the photograph, and can sustain a similar type of scrutiny itself.

These images are guaranteed to be things that the artist saw. They at the same time have a strong emotional undertow, because of the world they evoke. We know that what we see in her paintings must be predominantly her personal objects, places, and people. This gives the paintings the dimension of an autobiographical record, and suggests that some of them can be read as *memorabilia* of the artist's life. Each of them has the quality of an individual observation and event. In this way the paintings have a kinship with snapshots, by which we try to hold on to the memory of significant events in our lives.

In addition, there are a number of ways in which Mary Pratt's paintings clearly are visually quite other, and *more,* than the photograph. Although they follow their photographic sources closely, they bear the traces of her skills and decisions as a painter. The surface of the painted canvas is more richly textured and sensuous in colour than a photographic print ever could be. Qualities of light and colour relations, whether consciously or not, are often enhanced or subtly altered in ways that create aesthetic balance. These include the emphasis on a chosen pair of complementary colours (green and red, or blue and orange) that Pratt selects as the colour key for a particular painting. (Incidentally, we can never know in exactly what ways Mary Pratt's paintings do match the slides she works from: there are such differences of scale and lighting between them, and the slide image itself is so variable in size and illumination.)

The resulting enhancement and celebration of the image in Mary Pratt's paintings gives them a strongly affirmative quality. This goes some way towards countering the sense of absence and loss that the photograph evokes. The artist has rescued the desired image from its frail physical embodiment and has celebrated its power.

It is noteworthy that this negation of mortality is very often made in the face of subject matter that implicitly *is* concerned with death or with the fleetingness of time. Pratt chooses as her subject matter transitory states or moments of transition. She has unjustly been called a painter of food, of the kitchen. The visual presentation in no way distracts from the fact that here are dead fish, the carcasses of fowl and game, eggs that have been cracked and emptied. And it is visual contemplation rather than the active processes of food preparation that is emphasized. The treatment of Mary Pratt's subjects shows a focus on physical qualities (skin texture, anatomy, and the structure of particular tissue) that refer us back to their past functions in life. The intricately structured fish, the jewelled fruit, lie before us as sacrifices to human use; their moments are numbered.

In other paintings, elusive moments are picked on, which blatantly symbolize the transitory quality of life. A clear example of this is the very first painting Mary Pratt did from a photograph, and which established her mature painting project, *Supper Table* (1969). The raking late afternoon sun lights up the remains of a meal on the table which the family has just left: the peel of oranges, the parents' china teacups, the children's glasses, one of them still half-full of milk, the unclaimed hotdog, the open ketchup bottle stand as evidence of recent human presence. Or there are the *Fire Barrel* paintings (1981), flames against snow, the brief co-existence of mutually incompatible elements of heat and cold, or *Muriel Ferguson's Flag on the First of July* (1975), the flag spread out by the breeze with the sun shining through from behind, or *Entrance* (1979), a breakwater reflected in the sea at a rare moment of breathless calm without a ripple on the water. In some paintings, materials themselves take up strange and unrepeatable configurations such as *Cod Fillets on Tin Foil* (1974), *Cod Fillets on Cardboard Cartons* (1975), where extraordinarily chaotic forms are set off against symmetry. Finally, several paintings of wedding dresses are quintessential symbols of transitional moments in human life histories. The artist herself has commented repeatedly about her paintings that they are sights she has wanted to salvage from being forgotten.

One cannot help concluding that Mary Pratt's own choice of subjects introduces themes of mortality akin to those that haunt the photographic image. Her intense awareness of this struggles against it by elevating the fleeting image into the "eternal" language of painting. This is one of the sources of tension and paradox in her work. Pitting the conventions of photography against those of painting gives Mary Pratt's work some of its distinctive nuances of meaning.

◆

"Treat nature by the cylinder, the sphere, the cone…"

CÉZANNE (1904)

◆

"She will remain in the phenomenal world filled with ignorance with her sheep,
and not go with him."
JOYCE WIELAND (1983)

Pratt's initiation to painting came through art school in the Maritimes. There she would have become aware of the stylistic experiments of European avant-garde art, of the volcanic individuality of Picasso, of the severe abstraction of Mondrian, as remote (and by that time no longer novel) challenges to traditional art. But what was the relevance of such experiments to a student living in a predominantly rural part of Canada? The figurative tradition had remained strongly entrenched in North America, and the choices for most young artists in the early fifties, outside major art centres such as New York, would have been between different stylistic inflections that could be given to landscape, figure, or still life. Such stylistic options included expressive brushwork (Mary Pratt's exemplars here were Fritz Brandtner and Goodridge Roberts, both strong influences at the University of New Brunswick) or a style of drawing or a palette that could suggest a particular aesthetic sensibility (Alex Colville was a model here for the use of pale tones and geometrically structured figures which derived from the fresco and tempera painting of early Renaissance Italian masters). The paintings in Mary Pratt's graduation show, such as *Apples* (1960) shown on page 22, indicate her training equipped her to paint the subtly hued folds of white table-cloths and to place among them the apples of Cézanne.

In the second half of the fifties, however, abstraction made rapid headway in Canada. The Automatistes were well established by then, Painters Eleven had come together in 1954, and Vancouver boasted the surrealist biomorphism of Shadbolt and Binning. In 1956, a juried exhibition in Winnipeg, aiming to find "the best in Canadian art" startled its citizens with a predominantly abstract show.[2] The National Gallery of Canada simultaneously organized an exhibit of Canadian abstract art to go on tour. While the more sophisticated critics might question the too "easy elegance" and decorative superficiality of much of the new abstraction,[3] conservative critics doubted whether it was a valid idiom at all. Graham McInnes, in *Canadian Art,* deplored the "artistic heresy that condemns many of our painters to bootless variations on a theme essentially bleak." As a signpost to better horizons he illustrated a work by Alex Colville, *Woman, Man and Boat,* and called for "a deeper respect for human values and for that blending of the humanistic and the formal which, like a great battle, has swung back and forth over the field of painting for the last thousand years."[4]

These debates would have been followed with interest at Mount Allison, where Colville was a teacher and Mary Pratt and her future husband Christopher Pratt were students. The school prided itself on "providing the student with a sound, fundamental grounding of an academic nature before allowing him the widest freedom of individual expression," and also on instilling "an understanding and appreciation of the function and meaning of art in our time."[5] The principal at Mount Allison then was Lawren P. Harris, the son of pioneering Canadian abstractionist, Lawren Harris. He was himself a painter of hard-edged geometric abstractions, arrived at "through the gradual simplification of line and form in representational painting." Harris extolled the challenge of abstraction: "Being a relatively unexplored and unlimited field of creative expression, it is to me the most stimulating; it yields unexpected pleasures in the ideas it evokes and at the same time demands a greater degree of self-discipline."[6]

It was in this climate of debate — aware of the attractions and claims of abstraction, but also of the local constraints in an environment that valued discipline and tradition — that Mary Pratt received her training and watched her husband, Christopher Pratt, develop his own style. During the 1960s Christopher Pratt distilled a vision of the Newfoundland landscape that strongly emphasized abstract values. The austere forms of buildings and of bare hillsides and ocean were organized according to rigorous proportional systems involving Golden Sections rectangles. His paintings were statements of harmony and order as well as distillations of mood.

The problem for Mary Pratt was to find a language in which she could express her own interests. Her career was essentially on hold for some years while she raised their four small children, but whenever possible she made small oil paintings and rapid sketches of subjects that delighted her in and around the house: bread fresh from the oven, views from her windows, the shimmering colours of wildflowers in a meadow. It was the sensuous qualities of colour and light in the everyday world that attracted her. The only modern work with parallel concerns that she had seen, in reproduction, was that of the impressionists, but it had struck her as too "messy" to be a useful model for her own work. She had always been fascinated with the history of painting, and spent hours in her youth with the art books collected by her parents. Northern European still life and genre painting were her greatest love, particularly the seventeenth-century painter Georges de la Tour, with his solemnly lit figures, and the eighteenth-century painters Chardin and Boucher. When she finally realized that she could trap the fleeting appearances of light and coloured surfaces with the aid of the camera, she was ready to walk in the path of this primarily Northern European tradition.

Recently, scholars have re-examined the two contrasting painting traditions that were centred, one in Northern Europe, the other in Italy, since the Renaissance, and have pointed out some significant psychological and social dimensions of difference between them. These differences are so closely paralleled in the contrasting painting styles of Mary Pratt and Christopher Pratt that I will discuss them here.

The Northern tradition approached painting as a matter of describing the visible world in all its visual particularity, with attention to detail and surface. It developed the great technical possibilities of oil paint to render texture and luminosity. Its processes differed from those of Italian art, which at the time of the Renaissance was grounded by theorists like Alberti in intellectual systems for the reproduction of visible reality. The Italian systems were the laws of linear perspective, of chiaroscuro, of anatomy, and laws of composition and proportional harmony. These laws were subsequently codified and absorbed into the academic art training of European artists. The differences between the two traditions were recognized since the Renaissance by artists themselves. There is, for example, Michelangelo's famous dismissal of Flemish painting:

> It will appeal to women, especially to the very old and the very young, and also to monks and nuns and to certain noblemen who have no sense of true harmony. In Flanders they paint with a view to external exactness…They paint stuffs and masonry, the green grass of the fields, the shadow of trees…All of this, though it please some persons, is done without reason or art, without symmetry or proportion, without skilful choice or boldness.[7]

Svetlana Alpers has summed up the contrasting orientation of Italian Renaissance art as a "commanding attitude" towards the subject depicted, one that orders forms into relation with the frame and to a predetermined viewpoint, in which "sight or vision is defined geometrically," and that "concerns our measured relationships to objects in space rather than the glow of light or color."[8] Northern painters such as Vermeer, she argues, show the world "as if visual phenomena are present without the intervention of the human maker."

It has also been demonstrated that in the classical teachings of the Royal Academy, as typified by the *Discourses* of Sir Joshua Reynolds, the Italian mode of organizing perception was privileged as superior. Reynolds taught: "The whole of Beauty consists, in my opinion, in being able to get above singular forms, local customs, particular details of every kind."[9] Beauty is attained, according to him, not from copying nature, whose objects "upon close examination will be found to have their blemishes and defects," but from the intellectual discernment trained by "a long habit of observing what any sets of objects of the same kind have in common…This idea of the perfect state of nature, which the Artist calls Ideal Beauty, is the great leading principle, by which genius is conducted."[10]

Naomi Schor points out that in Western culture, and particularly in its academic teachings about art, the generalizing and abstracting mode of vision has normally been regarded as an elevated achievement, and ranked as superior and as masculine, while the particular, the detailed, has been labelled as a lower order and as feminine. The linking of different modes of art to masculinity and to femininity is not due to direct dictates of biology, but to the power of culturally defined social roles. Our gender roles are currently undergoing re-evaluation, which can be expected to affect the political judgements that spring from them, such as the privileging of particular modes of painting.

The work of Mary Pratt and of Christopher Pratt, however, seems to invite being subsumed under the two categories I have briefly outlined above. While Christopher Pratt refers in his paintings to buildings and landscape, he does so in a highly selective way, abstracting and paring down the depicted elements until they transcend their everyday existence and become symbols of an intellectual and poetic vision. This vision is conveyed through formal austerity and mathematical harmony. In Mary Pratt's work we are presented with material surfaces. She has stated, "The painters I like best are the seventeenth and eighteenth century genre painters, particularly Chardin. I'd like to do as well by textures like tin-foil and Saran Wrap as they did by cottons and linens."[11] She finds sensuous visual qualities in materials specific to our day: crumpled brown paper bags, plastic, modern casseroles and furniture, the play of light through venetian blinds.

Her paintings clearly reflect a domestic world, and this seems to connote a "feminine" vision. Doubly "feminine," one might conclude, since she chooses to work in what has been considered the humbler Northern mode, and to focus that vision onto her own experience as a woman. The objects she records in her paintings are snatched from the flux of domestic life, from the repetitive processes of food preparation, from the contingent fallout of family activity.

While the qualities shared with the Northern tradition can immediately be seen in Mary Pratt's paintings, the paintings are in fact also rigorously ordered in a number of ways, and this ordering gives them an added resonance of meaning. Her images contain everyday objects just as she has found them, but they are not presented in a casual way. From the classical, intellectual tradition Mary Pratt takes compositional devices such as the grid and the frame, economy and monumentality. Employing the camera lens, she brings objects parallel to the plane of the canvas. In this way she retains the respect for the flatness of the canvas that is characteristic of modern art. Her objects usually fill nearly the whole frame, allowing a minimum of distracting surrounding detail. She often places them centrally, or else in a dynamic asymmetry of contrasting flat areas. The underlying presence of a grid is asserted by lining up objects with the edges of the frame. The grid is also used explicitly in many images which involve the regular arrangement of identical forms, for example, in *Baked Apples on Tin Foil* (1969), in *Eviscerated Chickens* (1971), or *Eggs in an Egg Crate* (1975). Sometimes the objects are identical because they are manufactured articles, as in *Lunch Boxes* (1975), or *Preserves* (1978). Indeed, these two paintings, with their repetition and frontality, and their visual effects of surface reflection, even invite comparison with minimalist sculptor Don Judd, and his modular, industrially manufactured units.

In her work from 1969, through the seventies, Mary Pratt presented her images with a classical severity and economy, either surrounding them with luminous shallow space, or keeping background areas out of focus so that they become compositional elements rather than additional details. In the 1980s she has added elements of visual interest that have a greater complexity. The unfocused portions of the image take on a greater scale and emphasis as elements of abstract composition. This is seen in paintings such as *Blue Grapes and a Yellow Apple* (1984), and *Salmon Between Two Sinks* (1987). Here the central compositional motifs are rendered with greater plasticity than before. They are monumentally enlarged, and are counterbalanced by flattened background areas of colour and pattern that imply dark shadows and deep spaces behind the image.

In this mixture of the mundane and the visually sophisticated, Mary Pratt's work parallels that of the pop artists, who painted commercial imagery — Lichtenstein's comics, Andy Warhol's soup cans — but gave to it the rigorous composition and finish of 1960s abstraction. It has been pointed out that the pop artists combined elements from different visual codes — high art and advertising — in such a way as to make us freshly and strongly conscious of the operation of those codes.[12] Mary Pratt does something very similar by taking the formal language of classicizing artists such as Christopher Pratt and Alex Colville as the foil for her observation of everyday domestic objects. Her specific positioning in relation to the variety of art traditions on which she draws can thus be seen as a politics of the image. In her paintings she carries out an invasion of the realm of the ideal with the mundane, a subversion of its controlling authority with the assertion of the contingent and transitory elements of everyday life.

◆

"The fact is that until I saw paintings as icons, I couldn't see why
people painted at all."
MARY PRATT (1978)

I shall discuss now the associations opened up in Mary Pratt's work through her references to commercial art and to traditional and religious symbolism. These may seem to be two widely separated realms, but both contain myths that sustain our wish to transcend the limits of our daily lives. If we look at the components of her images, we find that often they weave together myths from the past with realities of the present.

Take, for example, that central image in her work, the fish. Roland Barthes has pointed out how certain foods can symbolize an entire culture. What could be a clearer emblem of the Maritimes than fish? In Mary Pratt's paintings these are as much icons of a local identity and of a state of mind as are the archetypal Newfoundland landscapes of Christopher Pratt.

The fish is also, as the artist herself has said, a biblical symbol: a token of salvation and of Christ's feeding of the multitude. It is a symbol of the bounty of nature. An undomesticated food source, fish are furnished by nature itself. Specifically, here they are a direct bounty to the individual, bypassing commercial transactions, since Pratt paints predominantly fish which are caught by anglers. Yet in her paintings the salmon and trout are shown in explicitly contemporary settings. They lie on steel sinks, plastic plates, Saran Wrap, asserting the promises of the past carried forward into the present.

Bread and fruit are other objects in her paintings that have counterparts in religious tradition. The dismembered moose and the fish pegged out to dry clearly invite reference to the Crucifixion. In addition, the solemnly composed presentation of these foods, taken from nature, has overtones of ritual. It suggests both sacrifice and grace before meat. It brings to mind, as a parallel, the Northwest Coast Indian ritual for placating salmon, by which, after the fish have been eaten, their bones are reverently returned to the sea.

There is also the ancient sacred symbolism of light which Pratt translates into modern secular settings. A long tradition in Christian art has associated light with Divine Grace, and, in the Northern European tradition that Pratt has espoused, effects of light have long been used as analogues of mood and of heightened significance. Mary Pratt is no longer an active church member, but she accepts this symbolism as a valid legacy that declares a sacred dimension in everyday things. She shares this concern with the sacred with other contemporary secular artists, particularly women, who are concerned with recapturing an awareness of human interdependence with nature.

In Mary Pratt's paintings, objects are displayed to the viewer in detailed, vividly coloured photographic close-up. This aspect is recognizably related to the mode of display in advertisements and women's magazines. It transports us at once to that world of comforting invitations to desire and to dream. Pratt has talked of the strong impression made on her in her youth by advertising imagery, of the pleasure it gave her through its heightened colour, its technical slickness, its emphasis on glossy surfaces, its evocation of luxury. So, when she felt it too "artsy" and unnatural to adopt the stylistic language of modernism for her own idiom, she turned to this shared North American heritage for grounding.

Advertising has played a formative role in North American society. It has been part of a popular Utopian myth, holding up glowing images, not only of material plenty, but of social transformation and of assimilation, to generations of immigrants to the New World.[13] It has been a very conspicuous and vigorous part of material culture in an environment that is not, like Europe, dominated by the monuments of the past. From the 1880s on, with the proliferation of reproductive processes such as photoengraving and chromolithography, commercial artists took pride in the thought that they could bring art to the people. Neoclassicism, art nouveau, art deco — a succession of aesthetically self-conscious styles dominated the applied arts. By the 1940s the photograph had become the visual basis of the advertising image, but this was an image manipulated in such a way as to amplify to the utmost the intensity of colour, the sparkle, the seductive material presence of the object. It spoke to practical good sense, and offered incontrovertible images of family security, of good health, of the promises of progress.

Mary Pratt's paintings are very visibly rooted in this North American visual heritage. She shares the democratic, optimistic urge of sixties artists to transcend the barriers between high art and popular culture and to make art out of a sophisticated reflection upon the latter. It was here that she found a viable context for representing children — *Doesn't That Look Just Like Our Anne* (1971), or *Barby with an Ice-Cream Cone* (1975) — and for celebrating everyday objects. But in transposing the advertising mode into the fine art medium, she goes on to complicate what looks familiar, to integrate unexpected levels of meaning.

◆

"Through simultaneous readings we fabricate Self as multiplicity. In the ambivalence of each picture's pleasures, we relinquish the singularity of a moral summit. There is no vantage point from which the truth of the image will be revealed." [14]
ANDREA FISHER (1987)

To enter a room where one of Mary Pratt's recent paintings of the female nude is hanging, is a disturbing experience. Take, for example, *This is Donna* (1987). The figure is life-sized, though her presence is so powerful that she seems larger than life. She stands with her back to the wall, poised to stride forward. With her weight on one foot and her hips tilted, her stance is the heroic pose of the classical male statue. The directness of her stare at the viewer has a hint of Michelangelesque *terribilità.* She stands to the left of the canvas' centre because the lighting as it has been set up projects her shadow, a bizarre green shape, on the wall to the right. This distorted shadow hints at hidden dimensions of human experience. The lighting itself, from both tungsten and fluorescent sources, interacts with the film's emulsion to bathe the figure in coloured reflections, which the painter has transposed to intense almost Matissian aquamarine shadows and orange lights.

There is a fundamental ambiguity in this image: is a woman in her underclothes credible as a Renaissance hero? Is this the defiant pose of an assertive woman or of a victim? These ambiguities are Mary Pratt's contribution to the painting of the nude. They spring from the application of her photo-realist style to a radically altered situation in painting. Her paintings of the female nude invade a domain which has been a masculine creation and prerogative. The female nude in Western art since the Renaissance has stood as a metaphor for beauty — beauty as commanded by the male gaze. The conventions for rendering the female figure were the product of the male artist's knowledge, of his idealization, of his power to command. Idealization of form or exotic narrative provided alibis for his, and the (male) viewer's, erotic pleasure. With the advent of modernism in the mid-nineteenth century, the painting of the female nude became an arena for the contestation of social conventions. Artists like Courbet and Manet refused to create classically idealized forms or mythological subjects. Their paintings of the female nude became paintings of real naked women, and divisive controversy resulted. Truthfulness to the artist's individual perceptions, whether objective or subjective, now became the alibi for the male gaze.

It is significant that in this early stage of the development of modern art, women artists could not paint equivalent subjects. Modernist painters like Manet, Degas, Picasso, when painting the nude in modern contexts, painted women who were recognizable by the viewer as women of "uncertain virtue." Berthe Morisot and Mary Cassat, brilliantly gifted women artists of the same generation could not, as Griselda Pollock has shown, undertake such a scrutiny of modern urban experience. Their gaze was controlled by what a middle-class woman was allowed to see.[15] Emily Carr internalized such prohibitions so deeply that at art school she refused to take life-classes.

When Mary Pratt was already a successful artist, she was asked why she did not paint the nude. Her reaction was, "Oh, I couldn't do that. That's for men to do. I wouldn't feel right."[16] But then she had second thoughts. Logically, it seemed to her that women above all should be interpreters of their own bodies. The male monopoly should be challenged. Instinctively she had understood that she was entering on masculine territory. Indeed, many contemporary feminist artists have refused representation of the nude female body on the grounds that the whole genre is still too loaded with its past function as an agency conditioning women into a psychic role of passivity and sexual subordination to men.

The opportunity for Mary Pratt to paint the female model came when her husband, Christopher, was throwing out photographic studies of the model which he no longer needed for his own painting. Mary Pratt decided to salvage them, and to select from them images that interested her. Her first choices produced simply elegant formal studies of the female body. She realized that she would have to define her own interests and desires for the image. These increasingly involved expressions of pleasure in female beauty, which deliberately included the character and agency of the woman model herself. The model was someone Mary Pratt had known for a period of years, first as an employee and subsequently as a friend. Pratt sought out images that showed the model's professional self-confidence, or which emphasized her assertiveness, her awareness of being looked at by a man. She went on as well to take her own photographs, arranging for the model to engage in normal daily activities, such as bathing or applying cosmetics, that would enable her to act spontaneously. To look at the most remarkable of these canvasses — *Girl in My Dressing Gown* (1981), *Girl in Red Turban* (1981), *Cold Cream* (1983), *Donna* (1986) — is actually to see a succession of different personae. Mary Pratt's images are neither images answering to male desire, nor to some essence of womanhood. They are images of masquerade.

The dimension of masquerade is hinted at as well in a series of paintings which Mary Pratt made in 1986 on the theme of marriage, and which were shown together under the title "Aspects of a Ceremony." Although the paintings are based on the weddings of her two daughters, they are not simply commemorations of family events. They are a scrutiny of such a ceremony as experienced today by specific people, a public not a private statement. Here again, Mary Pratt's concern for the contingent and for the detail lead her to breach representational conventions. The young brides who appear in these paintings assume by choice the ideals and stereotypes of the past, but they inhabit them with self-consciousness and ambivalence. The titles of the paintings assert complex situations, as do the representations themselves. *Barby in the Dress She Made Herself* (1986), for example, is the portrait of a bride in a pose familiar from informal eighteenth-century portraits. She is seated with her head and shoulders turning one way, her arms and legs the other, so as to show off her richly embroidered bodice. In a portrait such as Boucher's *Madame Pompadour,* this is a pose of flowing animation. Here, however, the expression on the bride's face and the tense clasping of her hands indicate that the psychological experience, the ceremonial dress, and the conventional pose are incommensurate elements.

◆

A tension between traditional symbols of the socially defined "feminine" role and a reality in which that role has shifted actually underlies all of Mary Pratt's paintings. It is this that makes divergent readings of her paintings possible. They can appear at first to be endorsements of a woman's traditional world, but a contradiction is apparent in the very conditions of their making. The artist has distanced herself from that world to make objects of use into objects of contemplation.

Ambiguities emerge in Mary Pratt's images as the result of her re-use of conventions — pictorial, photographic, commercial — in representing specific situations subject to time. During her career, different conventions have come to the fore as the chief focus of her attention. Her most recent work shows her bent on a new investigation, the exploration of an increasingly prominent handling of the painting medium itself. This comes as a surprise, since it is an element she had previously totally effaced from her work as "messy." Now we find conspicuous brushwork, bold manipulation of several media — watercolour, pastel, and charcoal — on a single surface, and the mingling of intensely coloured strokes to create optical mixtures of new and indeterminate hues. The photograph is still used to create a basic armature of fact, but over this is woven a fabric that calls attention to itself as artifice. The subjective and inventive responses of the artist are involved. In recent paintings such as *The Hall in My Mother's House,* Pratt evokes the spaces of her house, or even of her childhood, as explorations of emotion and memory. They are the latest developments in a painting project, which has always been an investigation of how the painter could respond to the constraints of particular conditions of vision. This demands a similar response from the viewer: the willingness to contemplate everyday sights as signs. In Mary Pratt's paintings they are signs of visual pleasure, but signs charged with conflicting currents of meaning from visual codes such as photography, advertising, fine art, and gender.

Gerta Moray

Grateful acknowledgement goes to Mira Godard and her staff for assistance with documentation, and to Cheryl Miyauchi for enlightening and enlivening discussions during the writing of this article.

1. Roland Barthes, *Camera Lucida, Reflections on Photography,* (New York: Noonday Press, 1981).

2. George Swinton, 'The Great Winnipeg Controversy,' *Canadian Art,* XIII No. 2 (1956), 244 – 49.

3. Swinton, 248.

4. Graham McInnes, "Has the Emperor Clothes?" *Canadian Art,* XIV No. 1 (1956), 13.

5. Douglas Lochhead, "Lawren P. Harris — A Way to Abstract Art," *Canadian Art,* XII No. 2 (1956), 67.

6. Lochhead, 66.

7. Svetlana Alpers, "Art History and its Exclusions: the Example of Dutch Art," in Norma Broude and Mary Garrard, eds., *Feminism and Art History,* (New York: Harper & Row, 1982), 194.

8. Alpers, 187.

9. Naomi Schor, *Reading in Detail,* (New York: Methuen, 1987), 11.

10. Schor, 15.

11. "Mary Pratt on Mary Pratt," *Mary Pratt: Paintings and Drawings,* (Memorial University of Newfoundland Art Gallery, 1975).

12. Lawrence Alloway, *American Pop Art,* (New York: Whitney Museum of American Art, 1974).

13. Stuart and Elizabeth Ewen, *Channels of Desire, Mass Images and the Shaping of American Consciousness,* (New York: McGraw-Hill, 1982), 47.

14. Andrea Fisher, *Let Us Now Praise Famous Women: Women Photographers for the U.S. Government, 1935 to 1944,* (New York: Routledge Chapman & Hall, 1987).

15. Griselda Pollock, *Vision and Difference,* (London: Routledge, 1988), 50 – 90.

16. Conversation with the artist, 6 March 1989.

PLATES

◆

This was our supper table back in 1968, when our oldest child was ten. Simple and honest, it was not "set up." It sat jumbled and untidy in its pool of autumn light, indicative of us.

SUPPER TABLE

◆

1969 24″ × 36″ OIL ON CANVAS
MARY AND CHRISTOPHER PRATT

40

The kitchen of my childhood had a first-class electric stove. In fact, it was so sparkling and up-to-date, that no matches were needed unless we wanted to singe the pin-feathers from a chicken or light the Christmas pudding. But in our early days at Salmonier, the kitchen was ruled by the eccentricities of this stove. The eccentricities were due entirely to my ignorance. I didn't know it had to be cleaned, so it blew up regularly and wouldn't bake bread or cake. It did, however, keep us warm. And on cold winter nights I sometimes look with disdain at my microwave oven and my clean little electric cooker, remembering the comforting heat of that wicked old oil stove.

OIL STOVE

◆

1969 18″ × 24″ OIL ON PANEL
PRIVATE COLLECTION

These apples are almost jewels, set in silver, gold, amber, and yet are obviously mundane, arranged in rows for "proper heat distribution," on tin foil for "easy clean up," redolent with cinnamon and cloves. They refuse to be boring – flaunting their romance despite every effort on my part to tear them from their history and their legends.

They cry to be celebrated, and so I painted them, exactly as my camera and I saw them.

BAKED APPLES ON TIN FOIL

◆

1969 16″ × 24″ OIL ON PANEL
NEW BRUNSWICK MUSEUM

44

I had baked myself a birthday cake, and put it on a plate to cool in the unheated "hen run" between the house and Christopher's studio. As I turned to shut the door, I realized that evidences of New Brunswick, where I was born, surrounded my cake: McIntosh apples from Keswick Ridge, potatoes from Hartland. A strange and touching coincidence.

CAKE, APPLES AND POTATOES

◆

1969   31⅛" × 20"   OIL ON GESSOED BOARD
MEMORIAL UNIVERSITY OF NEWFOUNDLAND

A fisherman from Placentia Bay was catching herring for the "Bait Service," and he brought me a bucket filled with these exquisite fish. They scattered like jewels on the plastic of the salt bag.

As he meticulously straightened them to lie in a neat row, he told me that they were part of the first unspoiled "catch" to be seen since the bay had been polluted with phosphorous the year before.

HERRING ON A SALT BAG

◆

1969   30″ × 21″   OIL ON PANEL

ARTHUR IRVING

This is the china that people gave me when I married Christopher. I thought it would look out of place in Salmonier, but it never has. Perhaps this proves that good design and good craftmanship are always a joy. And perhaps its presence has been a visible reminder of the formality of my childhood.

THE FLORENTINE

◆

1971 12″ × 16″ (APPROXIMATELY) OIL ON BOARD
MRS. W. J. WEST, FREDERICTON, NEW BRUNSWICK

50

Somebody had left the box on the kitchen floor — probably Mr. Tremblett, who had delivered it. As I bent to pick it up, the oranges and the paper bags filled my field of vision, the twisted paper, shining under the kitchen's 100 watt bulb. What had seemed to be labour — to store, to pay for, to cook, to serve, to clean up after — suddenly loosened as a wonder, something to keep forever, to paint.

BAGS

◆

1971 17 ¾″ × 24 ¾″ OIL ON GESSOED BOARD
MEMORIAL UNIVERSITY OF NEWFOUNDLAND

When I was a child, we bought chickens at an outdoor market, and pushed the breastbone and pinched the thigh and discussed youth and freshness. Later, my mother eviscerated the birds herself and burned off the pin-feathers with a candle flame.

As a bride, I did all that, once. Thereafter, I contented myself with frozen chickens, already cleaned and covered with some sort of yellow wax. However, I have never been able to entirely forget the barbarism of butchering. These "Sunday chickens," naked, empty, waiting on a Coca-Cola carton to be roasted, symbolized much about life in this civilization.

It was the first time I painted something that a lot of people didn't like.

EVISCERATED CHICKENS

◆

1971 18″ × 24 ¼″ OIL ON PANEL
MEMORIAL UNIVERSITY OF NEWFOUNDLAND

When my sister and I were children we were curly-haired, dimpled, and pretty. It was the era of Shirley Temple and Princess Elizabeth, the "age of the child." Drugstore calendars, magazine covers, and candy boxes were decorated with pictures of just such pretty children as my sister and me. My grandmother would often point to a calendar child, whose arms were filled with yellow chicks, or kittens, or puppies, and say, "Doesn't that look just like our Mary?"

When my Anne was three, she presented herself thus, in a trout stream, and, remembering my childhood, I turned her into a calendar child. To be professionally "correct," I took the painting to a commercial sign painter, and had the lettering done by him.

I suppose I really wanted an excuse to paint a baby. In the early seventies it was considered very soppy to paint a healthy child. By inflicting the formality of the printing, I managed to poke fun at the "child, symbol of innocent nature idea" and still produce a cheerful image of Anne.

DOESN'T THAT LOOK JUST LIKE OUR ANNE?

◆

1971 18″ × 24 ½″ OIL ON GESSOED BOARD
THE CANADA COUNCIL ART BANK, OTTAWA, ONTARIO

McDonald's
SALMONIER SERVICE
24 HOUR TOWING SERVICE · GREASE & OIL · TIRE REPAIR

		AUGUST			1968	
1968						
SUN	MON	TUES	WED	THU	FRI	SAT
					1	2
3	4	5	6	7	8	9
10	11	12	13	14	15	16
17	18	19	20	21	22	23
24/31	25	26	27	28	29	30

I am standing in the driveway of my father's house, looking down the street. The early morning sun is shining across the St. John River, through the elm trees and onto the faces of the houses. It is so familiar to me, so inevitable, that I never imagine carpenters building these houses. I assume they have "grown," like the trees, and have always been there, and will always be there.

FREDERICTON

◆

1972 29 ⅞″ × 46 ⅛″ OIL ON GESSOED BOARD
MRS. W. J. AYRE, FREDERICTON, NEW BRUNSWICK

58

Jelly is not particularly difficult to make, and it seems to be a civilized and wholesome accompaniment to meat. It is as necessary to our kitchen as bread and butter. Because it is so beautiful — such a clear and brilliant reminder of its origins — we treat it with the respect given to the major symbols in our culture. We set it, unmoulded and shimmering, on a crystal plate, transport it to the table with care, lay a silver spoon beside it, and stand back and consider the pleasure it gives us.

RED CURRANT JELLY

◆

1972 18″ × 18″ OIL ON GESSOED BOARD
NATIONAL GALLERY OF CANADA, OTTAWA, ONTARIO

When Dick Marrie shot his moose, he hung it, properly quartered, outside to season. When I saw it, against the snow — dark red, frozen, with little icicles of blood trickling down from it — I thought it looked wonderful. Aggressive, simple, necessary. The family's meat supply for the winter.

Only the small reflection of the carcass in the door window hint at a darker side to the image.

DICK MARRIE'S MOOSE

◆

1973 24″ × 18″ (APPROXIMATELY) OIL ON GESSOED BOARD
UNIVERSITY OF TORONTO, TORONTO, ONTARIO

"Quite a small salmon, but quite perfect."

"We'd never have kept it years ago."

"But the Salmonier River never did have a run of big fish."

"Perhaps. But only five pounds."

"Five pounds, six ounces."

This painting took nearly two years to complete. I had to discover a shorthand for plastic wrap, and I had to come to terms with how much "reality" really interested me.

Very easy now to discuss, very perplexing then to solve.

SALMON ON SARAN

◆

1974 18″ × 30″ OIL ON PANEL

PRIVATE COLLECTION

This is really not my image. I got it from a friend. He had been fishing, and after considering the days' catch, was about to carry the bucket full of fish home. Then, as he said, "I looked down at those fish, and I thought about you." He photographed them and brought me the slide. I was quite surprised that he had done this. I hadn't realized that he had ever really looked at my paintings.

TROUT IN A BUCKET

◆

1974 24″ × 30″ (APPROXIMATELY) OIL ON GESSOED BOARD
D. PIPPSEY

Cod fillets, coated with salt and pepper, paprika and flour — tossed in a curve of tin foil — a very ordinary sight in many kitchens. Essential if the fish is to be fried. We deal with this sort of stuff every day, hardly seeing what we do, always thinking one step ahead of what we're doing.

Sometimes an image like this stops us, and we see humble food, wrapped in its history, central to our culture. The Cod Wars, treaties between nations, the building of fishing fleets, the industry supporting economies, feeding millions. Perhaps the foil should have been gold.

COD FILLETS ON TIN FOIL

◆

1974 21″ × 26 ¾″ OIL ON GESSOED BOARD
DR. AND MRS. A. BRUNEAU, ST. JOHN'S, NEWFOUNDLAND

It is possible to get very good frozen fish now. However, twenty years ago, freezing and storing processes were not well controlled, and dry, tasteless fish emerged from the cartons on the freezer shelf. To those of us who knew the taste and texture of fresh cod, these tortured fillets were a sad sacrifice.

COD FILLETS ON CARDBOARD CARTONS

◆

1975 19 ½″ × 28 ¾″ OIL ON PANEL
ART GALLERY OF ONTARIO, TORONTO, ONTARIO

70

I had made an extravagant birthday cake, one that required a dozen eggs. As I broke the eggs, I simply put the shells back into the egg crate, intending to close the lid and throw everything into the garbage. However, the light shone on the slippery interior of the empty shells, and the light sank into the porous papier-mâché egg crate, and the textures and colours combined to create an image symbolic of life and abandoned life. I, who had recently failed to bring twin sons to term, felt the importance of the image.

EGGS IN AN EGG CRATE

◆

1975 20″ × 24″ OIL ON PANEL
MEMORIAL UNIVERSITY OF NEWFOUNDLAND

A young girl from St. Vincent's asked if she could get married in our garden. The night before the wedding she brought her wedding dress to the house so that it would be unwrinkled for the ceremony.

The day dawned bright and clear, and when I opened the door of the room where she would get ready, I saw the dress, glowing in reflected sun. It was simple and entirely without artifice. For a few minutes the intricacies of my life fell away, and I believed I could be uncomplicated.

WEDDING DRESS

◆

1975 45 ½″ × 23″ OIL ON PANEL
PRIVATE COLLECTION, NEW BRUNSWICK

I wanted to do a painting of an ice-cream cone held out as an offering. It was an image remembered from my own childhood, and I thought it might make an interesting painting. My daughter and I worked away for some time, trying to get the right "look." However, as usually happens when I try to set up a situation, nothing magic happened, so I told her to eat the ice-cream before it melted. As she stuck out her tongue to catch the drip the magic happened.

BARBY WITH AN ICE-CREAM CONE

◆

1975 23 ¾" × 23 ⅝" OIL ON PANEL
DOFASCO INC., HAMILTON, ONTARIO

Before I came to Newfoundland, my experience of "trifle" was mostly literary: a British dessert with custard and sherry and sponge-cake. "Not very nice," I thought. I was wrong, it is nice, as good as the cook.

I was not the cook in this case. This trifle was made by a friend whose English mother had ordained that slices of sherry-soaked raspberry roll be held in place with raspberry Jell-O. The dessert was the final course at a party that my brother-in-law attended, and remembering that I had often said that a trifle would make a good painting, he had photographed this for me.

At first I wasn't very enthusiastic about the image. I had really wanted a more complex bowl and a more exotic swirl of whipped cream. However, there was something haunting about the foolish little table set in a darkening garden, full of white clover, mysterious with dark shadows and distant hedges, something akin to British mystery stories.

THE TRIFLE IN THE GARDEN

◆

1975 27 ½″ × 25″ OIL ON PANEL
DR. P. CHAPNICK, TORONTO, ONTARIO

Muriel Ferguson was the leader of the Senate for some time, and when she retired, the city of Fredericton celebrated her accomplishments with a day of festivities. Muriel decorated her house with flags. On the First of July, her house was already decorated, a confident declaration of unabashed nationalism.

MURIEL FERGUSON'S FLAG ON THE FIRST OF JULY

◆

1975 23″ × 36″ OIL ON PANEL
CALVERT C. PRATT, SR., NEWFOUNDLAND

When we lived in Glasgow, the air was so full of soot that I couldn't hang the washing outdoors at all. We had to dry everything — diapers, shirts, socks — in front of a tiny gas fire. Since then, every line of clothes, shining in the clear light of morning, has reminded me of how insidious pollution is, and of how wonderful the world can be.

SUMMER CLOTHES

◆

1975 15″ × 24″ OIL ON PANEL
MRS. J. K. PRATT, NEWFOUNDLAND

82

*The pond is very flat and very dark in September. I used to think it was just the contrast
from days of children splashing about, keeping the water in a state of constant turmoil,
to days when they were in school. However, now that the children are grown and gone,
I still see the dark, flat, secret mirror of the September pond, and when I stand at its edge
and look down, I feel that if I were to fall in I'd keep falling forever.*

CHILDREN'S WHARF IN SEPTEMBER

◆

1975 20 ½″ × 25″ OIL ON PANEL
DR. AND MRS. J. T. DUNNE

84

When I first started painting from slides, I worried a lot about the areas of the image that were not in focus. Sometimes I had several slides all of the same image and lighting, but with various focal settings. Then, if I chose, I could keep the entire image in focus.

I found I didn't like seeing everything "sharp." It was boring and less selective. I wanted the ambiguity that allowed for a sense of space and time and gave the eye an undefined area in which to move.

JUNE GERANIUM

◆

1976 16″ × 24″ OIL ON PANEL
MR. AND MRS. G. MacNEILL, TORONTO, ONTARIO

To paint a roast beef simply because it represents obvious things — the parcelled flesh of a slaughtered animal, man's greedy appetite, Sunday dinner — would probably not be enough reason for me. This roast, surrounded by light and suspended on a fragile rack, displayed "other" qualities.

ROAST BEEF

◆

1977 16 ½″ × 22 ½″ OIL ON PANEL
LONDON REGIONAL ART GALLERY, LONDON, ONTARIO

Once when I was showing some slides of my work, a lady asked me why I called this painting Steamed Pudding. *It hadn't occurred to me to call it anything else, because there was a pudding inside the bowl, and because of the tin foil "cover" and the string, I figured everyone would know about the pudding.*

STEAMED PUDDING

◆

1977 22″ × 22″ OIL ON PANEL
PRIVATE COLLECTION, OTTAWA, ONTARIO

These preserves were a gift from a friend.

PRESERVES

◆

1978 13″ × 16 ½″ OIL ON PANEL

PRIVATE COLLECTION, TORONTO, ONTARIO

A friend brought us this smoked arctic char from Labrador. It had been wrapped in waxed paper and brown paper. I unwrapped it on the front porch. The various lines and textures of floor, papers, and fish made the image complex graphically and gave it a dry, thin, mathematic quality that seemed entirely appropriate for dried fish.

ARCTIC CHAR

◆

1978 24″ × 24″ OIL ON PANEL
DAVID P. SILCOX, TORONTO, ONTARIO

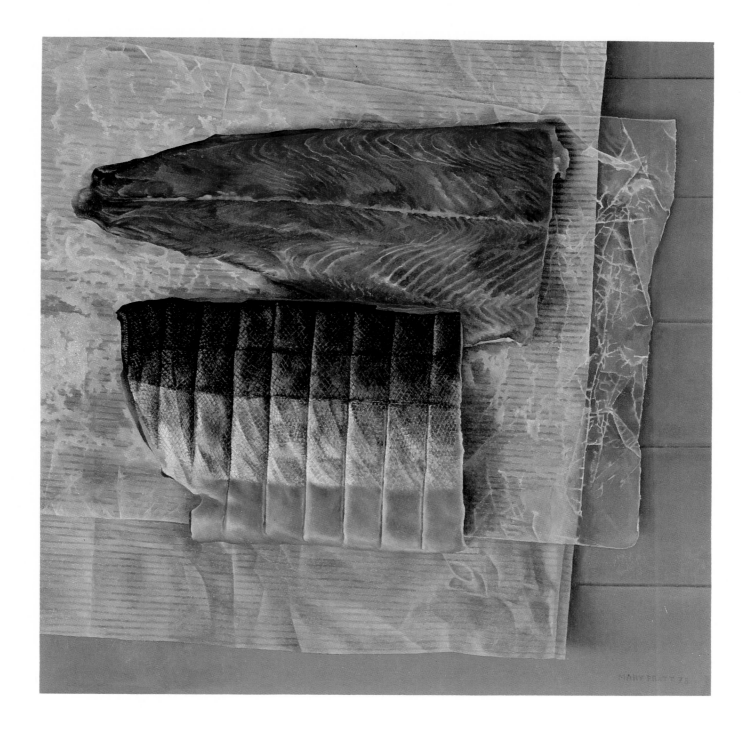

Images like this are fairly common in rural Canada. The moose hung up to cure, surrounded by farm machinery or any other paraphernalia that people keep in out-buildings. The man who killed this moose owned a service station, and he simply hoisted the carcass onto the back of his wrecking truck.

Knowing that I painted fish and chickens and other dead and bleeding creatures, he kindly asked me if I'd like to see his moose.

He is a good businessman. He has brought up a family of seven. He and his wife run a neat little shop. They are our neighbours.

He had no idea that I would be upset by this moose. But to me it screamed "murder, rape, clinical dissection, torture," all the terrible nightmares hanging right in front of me.

I couldn't understand why he hadn't thought of all that.

SERVICE STATION

◆

1978 40″ × 30″ OIL ON PANEL
PRIVATE COLLECTION, TORONTO, ONTARIO

This painting is the first in a series I've done over the past ten years of Donna Meaney.

Donna came to live with us when she was seventeen, after she had graduated from the local high school. She was very tiny, but beautifully built. She helped me around the house, baby-sat the children, and was Christopher's model.

The photograph for this painting was taken by Christopher. I did the painting quite a few years after Donna left us. Christopher preferred to work from the model, and since Donna wasn't available, he said that all his photographs were useless to him. I didn't know whether to believe him or not, but this particular image seemed too perfect to throw away.

When I painted it, I was aware that she was looking at Christopher, not me, and this difficult knowledge has continued to plague me, as I've worked on other photographs offered to me over the years.

GIRL IN A WICKER CHAIR

◆

1978 33″ × 33″ OIL ON BOARD
PRIVATE COLLECTION

Models "at rest" always seem to be preoccupied with some minor problem or defect in their person: a small blemish on the elbow or knee cap or a toe nail that needs attention. Also, the more relaxed or graceful the pose, the more contorted the attitude "at rest." Donna was "resting," on a kitchen chair.

NUDE ON A KITCHEN CHAIR

◆

1979 39 ¼″ × 29 ¼″ OIL ON PANEL
PRIVATE COLLECTION, TORONTO, ONTARIO

A grilse is a young salmon, and these were caught in the river that flows around the curve of our front lawn. We usually steam salmon whole, or fry it in steaks. A very thin portion was required this time for the barbecue, so my daughter split them. She later became a professional cook, and when she sees this painting she despairs that she didn't do a very neat job. I despaired too as the jagged edges of the flesh were rather difficult to paint. However, had they been perfect, I might not have found them very interesting to look at.

SPLIT GRILSE

◆

1979 22 ½″ × 25 ¼″ OIL ON PANEL
WYNICK/TUCK GALLERY, TORONTO, ONTARIO

Summer fish used to lie like this — head to tail to head to tail — in neat rows drying in the sun. Those spindly dying "flakes," constructed impossibly against the cliffs reminded me of alters to some god. The fish, split and splayed were like mutilated offerings.

SUMMER FISH

◆

1979 26″ × 30″ OIL ON PANEL
PRIVATE COLLECTION, TORONTO, ONTARIO

104

All of these rocks were "blasted." You can see the marks of the blasting rods.
A man-made breakwater, a mechanical light house.

ENTRANCE

◆

1979 34″ × 48″ OIL ON PANEL
BEAVERBROOK ART GALLERY, FREDERICTON, NEW BRUNSWICK

One weekend we sailed our boat to Brigus and explored the little lanes and backyard gardens of the town. Roses and columbines, peonies and sweet rocket, gooseberry bushes and raspberry canes all vaguely untidy, but comfortable and prosperous, and divided by picket fences marching in all directions.

The sun shone, the church bells rang, and as we crossed a bridge spanning a river emptying into the sea, I looked down. Almost directly under me was this boat, it's interior whitewashed and divided to hold fish, looking like a whale, with its bones all bleached and obvious.

TIED BOAT

◆

1980 18″ × 18″ OIL ON PANEL
PRIVATE COLLECTION, TORONTO, ONTARIO

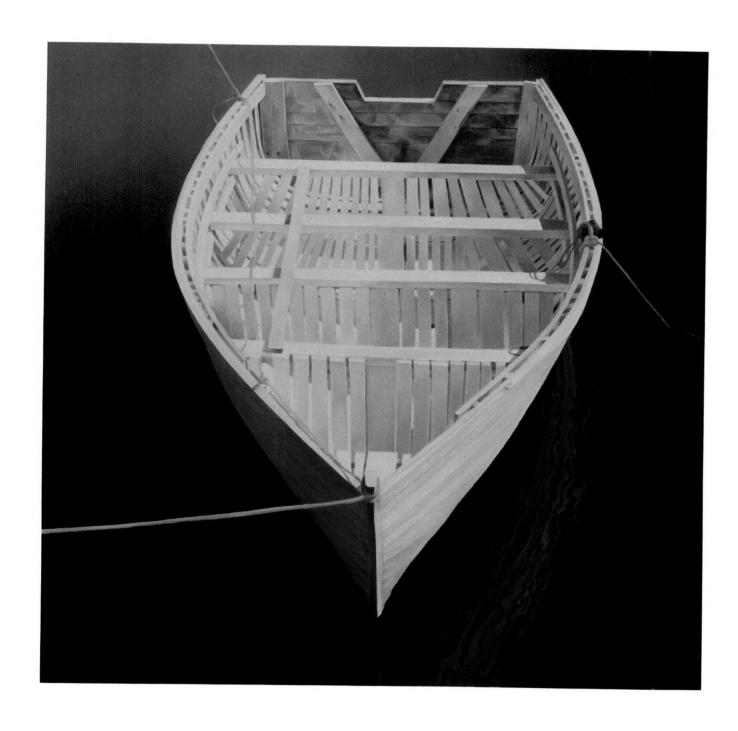

When my children were young, I cooked the Christmas turkey in a tin-foil tent. That way I could spend my time with the family and not worry about the main course of the meal of the year. Apparently my friends did the same thing, because when they saw this painting (which I thought might well be ambiguous) they all said, "What a wonderful turkey."

CHRISTMAS TURKEY

◆

1980 18″ × 23 ½″ OIL ON PANEL

ROBERT McLAUGHLIN ART GALLERY, OSHAWA, ONTARIO

All three gifts were from my mother-in-law. The lace table-cloth, the glass bowl, and the fruit. It is one of the last days of Christmas, and the fruit that is left in the bowl has shrunk and settled. Probably it's a little soft. I liked the "old" look, rather mellow compared with some brash things I sometimes paint.

THREE GIFTS

◆

1981 26″ × 30″ OIL ON PANEL
PRIVATE COLLECTION, TORONTO, ONTARIO

112

One can be profound about Fire and Ice:
"Some say the world will end in fire;
Some say in ice.
From what I've tasted of desire
I hold with those who favor Fire." — Robert Frost

Or one can be flippant, and recall Revlon's famous lipstick of the fifties, Fire and Ice,
"makes blues bluer and reds redder." When I was in high school we all wore it.

This old barrel is our "burning barrel." Every morning we burn yesterday's mistakes
from the studios.

FIRE BARREL

◆

1981 26″ × 18″ OIL ON PANEL
CALVERT C. PRATT, SR., NEWFOUNDLAND

The wrapping papers and packing boxes, the tapes and ribbons and stickers rise from the burning barrel in a column of flames. The magic of a bonfire becomes heavy with ritual as grown-ups watch from the living-room windows, and wait impatiently for dinner.

CHRISTMAS FIRE

◆

1981 30″ × 23 ½″ OIL ON BOARD
LAVALIN INC., TORONTO, ONTARIO

The bowl is packed tight with fruit. Unlike Three Gifts, *which was painted earlier,
this image isn't meant to make any allusions to past feasts or previous encounters.
It is simply meant to celebrate.*

BOWL'D BANANA

◆

1981 24″ × 20″ OIL ON GESSO ON PANEL
RICHARD AND SANDRA GWYN, LONDON, ENGLAND

117

One snowy day in February, Donna and I were trying to find some images of a young woman coping with her appearance. It was one of the first times I took the photographs myself.

The timeless gestures all appeared. This was one of them.

GIRL IN RED TURBAN

◆

1981 24″ × 20″ OIL ON PANEL
PRIVATE COLLECTION, TORONTO, ONTARIO

I asked Christopher to take some slides of Donna in a satin gown. I had planned to buy her one, thinking how splendid she would look, but I didn't manage to get into town. Consequently, she wore mine. It was too big for her, and hung straight from her shoulders. It hadn't been pressed, and the resulting pictures had a rumpled, sulky look that I hadn't expected. Once again, she was looking at Christopher. This wasn't the image I had intended, but I accepted it anyway.

GIRL IN MY DRESSING GOWN

◆

1981   60 ½" × 30 ½"   OIL ON PANEL
J. RON LONGSTAFFE, VANCOUVER, BRITISH COLUMBIA

It is difficult for me to paint a person if that person is looking out of the painting at me. There is almost no freedom to think of the person in a general way. She becomes an individual, with her own persona. The whole painting begins to serve that persona, and gradually any ideas I might have had about the image dissolve, and I give way to a portrait.

IN THE BATHROOM MIRROR

◆

1983 42″ × 26″ OIL ON BOARD

BRASCAN CORPORATION

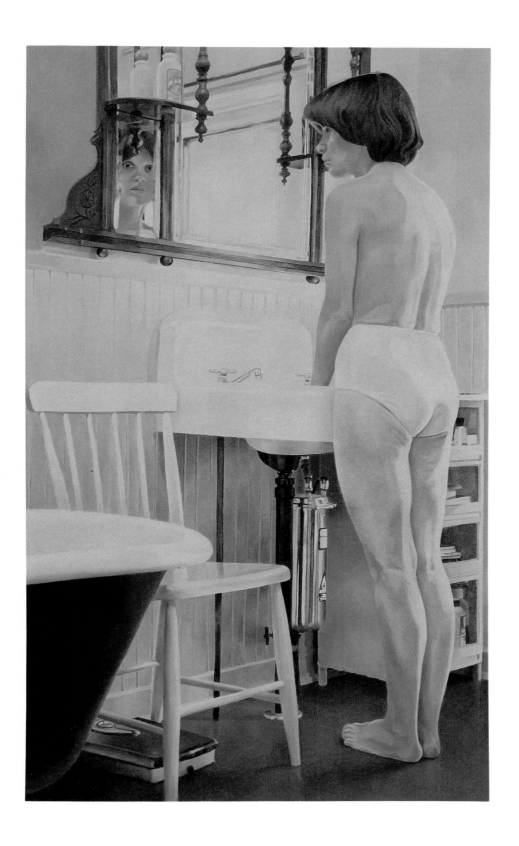

I wanted to see what the skin would look like emerging from the intense, almost opaque, blue of bath water full of bath salts. What Donna presented, however, was playfulness, not at all what I'd had in mind. Her body gleamed almost pearlescent against the dark blue; she kicked the water to swirl in froth around her. She forgot the camera. I didn't try to inflict my preconceived ideas on this spontaneity. I became what the viewers of the painting would become, a voyeur.

BLUE BATH WATER

◆

1983 67″ × 45 ¼″ OIL ON BOARD
PRIVATE COLLECTION, TORONTO, ONTARIO

Donna's face emerging from layers of face cream. You can see where she has pulled her fingers across her forehead, her intensity giving the cream the same lines she has in her skin.

I hardly used any paint at all, most of the white is underpainting gesso.

Usually I don't allow myself this "painterly" technique. Unless the image is powerful, it only says "technique" anyway.

COLD CREAM

◆

1983 19″ × 14″ OIL ON GESSOED BOARD
CANADA COUNCIL ART BANK, OTTAWA, ONTARIO

This is Katherine, my first grandchild, having her first bath. She is hardly a week old. Her hands are still curled up, her head is quite large.

But she is not afraid. Rather, she is fascinated by the drops of water she has kicked up and she takes her security for granted.

CHILD WITH TWO ADULTS

◆

1983 21 ½″ × 21 ½″ OIL ON GESSOED BOARD
PRIVATE COLLECTION, TORONTO, ONTARIO

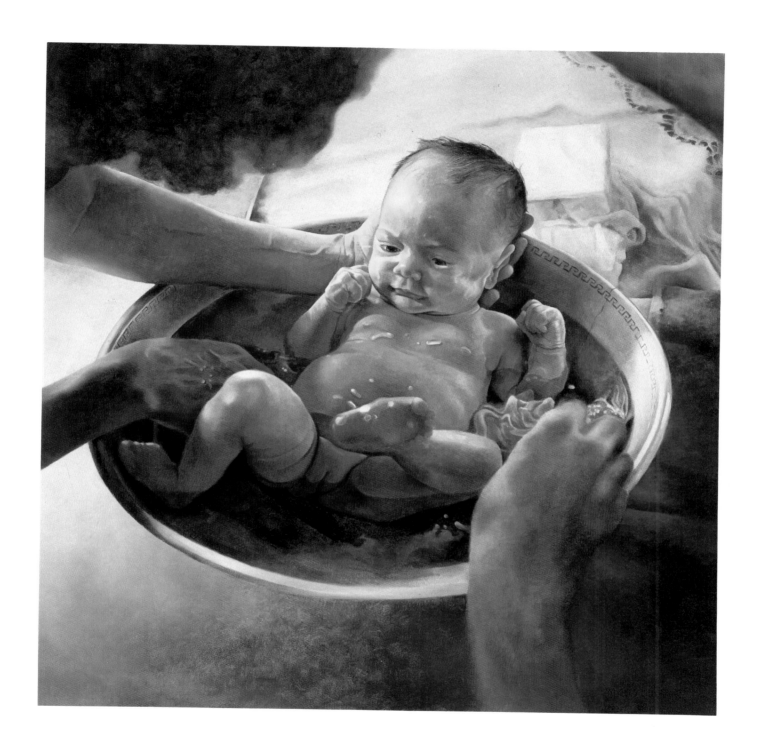

130

Eggs don't lie like this, all light and weightless. When eggs are really eggs, and not just the shells of eggs, they are heavy and will only lie so that the protected yolk is balanced. These eggs have been blown, and will eventually be painted and hung on a budding branch from the peach-leafed willow to please children on Easter Sunday.

The symbolism here is all wonderful, but it was the image itself that caught me: the dark blues and purples, the thin light, the weightlessness, the paper towel.

HOLLOWED EGGS FOR EASTER

◆

1983 30″ × 36″ (APPROXIMATELY) OIL ON GESSO ON MASONITE PANEL
ACADIA UNIVERSITY, WOLFVILLE, NOVA SCOTIA

One day when Donna was posing for me, it had been snowing for a day and a night, and the house was banked with drifts on three sides. We seemed to be entirely isolated. It was very quiet, and the light was wonderful, not bright, but everywhere, filtered by the still falling snow.

Donna was standing by the window, when she was suddenly aware that a white cat camouflaged by the snow was staring at her.

WHITE CAT ON FRONT PORCH

◆

1984   21 ½″ × 29 ⅞″   OIL ON BOARD
PRIVATE COLLECTION, LONDON, ONTARIO

A fish that is laid in a bowl curls around inside the bowl, and retains some of his dignity, even though he is really no longer alive. But a fish that is zipped into a plastic bag loses all his mystery and all his grace.

TROUT IN A ZIPLOCK BAG

◆

1984 20″ × 24″ (APPROXIMATELY) OIL ON BOARD

VANCOUVER ART GALLERY, VANCOUVER, BRITISH COLUMBIA (GIFT OF J. RON LANGSTAFFE)

136

This painting was difficult. The pomegranates were hidden by the heavy crystal and the thin colours shattered and reflected and re-reflected from one intricate surface to another. However, since my eyes could see them, I assumed that I could paint them. Sometimes I seem to be two people. One who does not paint and one who does. The one who does not paint assumes that the one who does can paint anything. The one who is the painter sometimes finds it difficult to live up to that faith.

POMEGRANATES IN A CRYSTAL BOWL

◆

1984 26″ × 30″ (APPROXIMATELY) OIL ON GESSO ON BOARD
CANADA PACKERS

I was lying on the grass beside the garden table. When I turned my head to look up, the fruit in the bowl looked enormous, fat, bursting almost. The day was extremely clear, the colours exaggerated and very bright. It wouldn't have worked at all without that deep shadow under the table.

BLUE GRAPES AND A YELLOW APPLE

◆

1984 24″ × 26″ OIL ON MASONITE

PRIVATE COLLECTION, TORONTO, ONTARIO

This casserole was made in England, but its inspiration was oriental. When I saw it in the microwave oven, lit by a light so orange that it turned all the whites aqua, it acquired a life of its own. Besides, the oven made a niche, frightening in its potential.

ROMANCING THE CASSEROLE

◆

1985 20″ × 28″ OIL ON BOARD
ARTIST

It had long been a plan of mine to paint a wedding dress pinned onto a clothes-line. Waiting for the right day, the right dress, the right clothes-line turned into a long story of procrastination.

After Anne was married, she brought her dress down to Salmonier to air it out before packing it away. Not wanting to let the train trail in the wet grass, she hung it on a small maple tree, catching the pearled train loop on a twig.

This image, at once luminous and sacrificial, was far better than what I'd had in mind to arrange.

WEDDING DRESS

◆

1986 29 ¼″ × 22 ½″ OIL ON BOARD
PRIVATE COLLECTION, VANCOUVER, BRITISH COLUMBIA

During the spring when Anne was married, she was in university studying The Faerie
Queen. *She wanted her dress to look Elizabethan, and the ceremony to be traditional.
Since she had never been to a wedding, she had no model to copy. I found this desire
for ritual and history interesting.*

*As she walked through my garden, she looked like a pre-Raphaelite heroine, but overhead
is the telephone wire, and the simple window frames on the house betray
the late-twentieth century.*

ANNE IN MY GARDEN

◆

1986 30″ × 26″ OIL ON BOARD
PRIVATE COLLECTION, VANCOUVER, BRITISH COLUMBIA

This is my daughter Barbara in her wedding dress.

BARBY IN THE DRESS SHE MADE HERSELF

◆

1986   35 ¾″ × 23 ¾″   OIL ON BOARD
PRIVATE COLLECTION, OTTAWA, ONTARIO

This painting was part of a show I put together called "Aspects of a Ceremony"
that concerned weddings.

The first thing I thought of when I woke up on my wedding day was, "Will the sun shine
on me?" I wanted to paint the first light of morning, and I watched all summer –
hoping for the perfect first blush of light.

It wasn't until I'd finished the painting and sent it to my dealer that it occurred to me
that I had finally painted a landscape.

THE MORNING

◆

1986 30″ × 45″ OIL ON BOARD
COURTESY OF EQUINOX GALLERY, VANCOUVER, BRITISH COLUMBIA

150

She came to Newfoundland, the bride of a philosopher and theologian, and posed for me in her wedding dress which was very old, from a different time. She had come from Harvard, where she had been pursuing a doctorate in Ancient Chinese Literature.

STUDENT OF ANCIENT CHINESE LITERATURE

◆

1986 29 ½" × 37" OIL ON BOARD
PETRO-CANADA

This speaks about the pleasure of a young woman's involvement with cosmetics.

DONNA WITH A POWDER PUFF

◆

1986 22″ × 13 ¾″ OIL ON BOARD

COURTESY OF EQUINOX GALLERY, VANCOUVER, BRITISH COLUMBIA

After painting women with no clothes for several years, I ceased to consider them helpless. It has been a tradition to consider the naked woman as vulnerable.

While I understand this reasoning, I prefer to think that women who have abandoned their clothes have also abandoned layers of artifice. I noticed the marks left from the elastic in her knee socks.

DONNA

◆

1986 35 ½″ × 27 ½″ OIL ON BOARD
MEMORIAL UNIVERSITY OF NEWFOUNDLAND

One male trout — one female. Christopher caught them within minutes of each other, as they swam up the river together at the end of the summer, when the river was empty of salmon, children, and boats.

TWO TROUT

◆

1986 22 ¾″ × 33 ½″ OIL ON MASONITE
PRIVATE COLLECTION, TORONTO, ONTARIO

Sure of herself, seductive, she looks at Christopher who is clicking the shutter. I was touched by the marks of the buttons on her stomach and the impressions of stitches and zipper left by her jeans.

GIRL IN GLITZ

◆

1987   30″ × 45 ¼″   OIL ON MASONITE
ART GALLERY OF ONTARIO, TORONTO, ONTARIO

When I first knew Donna she was only seventeen. This is the latest painting I've done of her, some 20 years later. I hoped to indicate the strength that has sustained her over many turbulent years.

THIS IS DONNA

◆

1987 73″ × 42″ OIL ON CANVAS

JIM COUTTS, TORONTO, ONTARIO

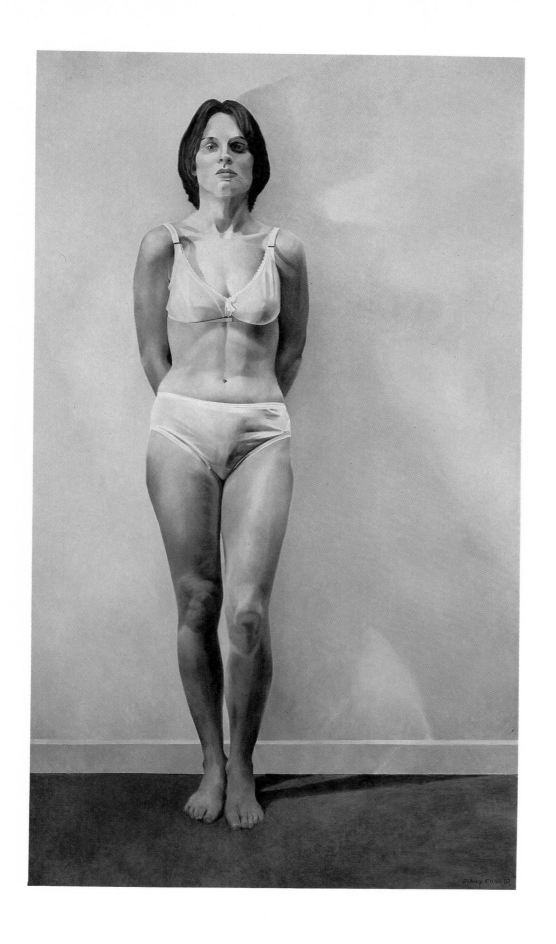

This was the original Salmon on Saran, *laid on tin foil and Saran Wrap. The photography had been forced and unsuccessful – so I changed the foil to red when I did the painting.*

SILVER FISH ON CRIMSON FOIL

◆

1987 18 ⅜″ × 27 ⅜″ ACRYLIC ON MASONITE
PRIVATE COLLECTION, TORONTO, ONTARIO

I was about to cut the head of this salmon, when he slipped out of my hand and landed on the ledge dividing the two sinks. Bars of light streaming in between the slats on the venetian blind banded him, and for a moment he looked as if he were still in a pool, circled with light, leaping into the sun.

SALMON BETWEEN TWO SINKS

◆

1987   28 ½″ × 42 ¼″   OIL ON MASONITE

PRIVATE COLLECTION, EDMONTON, ALBERTA

*Quite a large painting — I did it for fun, enjoying all the red, the turquoise slashes,
the larger areas of pink, and the fish itself.*

DECKED MACKEREL

◆

1987 36″ × 54 ¾″ OIL ON BOARD
THE MANUFACTURERS LIFE INSURANCE COMPANY, TORONTO, ONTARIO

Shasta daisies, summer mallow and monkshood — Katherine is bringing us a present.
She is a gift herself, but she may never figure that out.

CHILD BRINGING FLOWERS

◆

1987 24 ½″ × 35 ⅜″ OIL ON MASONITE
PRIVATE COLLECTION, SARNIA, ONTARIO

I wanted to paint a body emerging from the depths of our peat-brown river into the sun.
I did drawings and planned designs, but the real thing was much more wonderful.
I hadn't realized that the sun would continue to wrap the body, even under the water.

VENUS FROM A NORTHERN POND

◆

1987   25 ½″ × 32″   OIL ON MASONITE

ARTIST

This was our bed in the morning sun.

BEDROOM

◆

1987 45″ × 38″ OIL ON MASONITE
PRIVATE COLLECTION, TORONTO

174

The careless slap and dash of mixing a water-base medium with a waxy medium allowed me to make this bonfire work. It is not the classic image of a bonfire with flames, sparks, and smoke deliberately considered and carefully executed. Rather, it is an image as fluting and ephemeral as a bonfire really is.

BONFIRE BY THE RIVER

◆

1988   49 ½″ × 33 ¾″   MIXED MEDIA ON PAPER

PRIVATE COLLECTION, VANCOUVER

Someone suggested that perhaps the background was a bit black for the fragile, emerging leaves. However, I had put the bowl on the hearth in front of the Franklin stove, and when the pale green leaves began to curl out of the bulbs, they looked so wonderfully innocent against the cast iron that I couldn't very well move them.

PAPERWHITES IN CRYSTAL ON TIN FOIL

◆

1988 35″ × 46″ MIXED MEDIA ON PAPER
PRIVATE COLLECTION, VANCOUVER

*Most pomegranates are rough and quite irregular. These weren't. They were a bit
textured, but remarkably perfect and brilliantly red. The most beautiful pomegranates
I had ever seen.*

POMEGRANATES IN A CRYSTAL BOWL

◆

1988   44 ¾″ × 37 ½″   MIXED MEDIA ON PAPER
PRIVATE COLLECTION, VANCOUVER, BRITISH COLUMBIA

In the summer, the drapes and blinds were closed to keep out the heat. Here the front door is open and the morning light, already sultry with heat, floods through. Beyond is the St. John River.

THE HALL IN MY MOTHER'S HOUSE

◆

1989 47″ × 31″ MIXED MEDIA ON PAPER

PRIVATE COLLECTION, VANCOUVER

List of Plates

◆ ————————————————————

Biography

1935	Born Fredericton, New Brunswick, on March 15 to William J. West and Katherine (McMurray) West.
1939	Kindergarten.
1941	Enrolled in grade one, Charlotte Street School, Fredericton. Art lessons in every grade.
1946	Painting accepted in an international show of children's painting, The Luxembourg Museum, Paris.
1947	Studied painting with Lucy Jarvis, Fredericton.
1949	Graduated into Fredericton High School.
1950	Studied painting with John Todd, Fredericton, and with Fritz Bantner at summer school, U.N.B.
1951	Studied at U.N.B. summer with Alfred Pinsky and met Ghitta Caisserman.
1953	Graduated from Fredericton High School. Developed an arts program for city playgrounds, Fredericton. Enrolled in the Mount Allison School of Fine Arts. The teachers were Lawren Harris (Head of the School), Alex Colville, and Ted Pulford.
1955	Christopher Pratt helps me with sets for a Noel Coward play.
1956	Receive a certificate in Fine Arts, Mt. Allison. Get a job as an occupational therapist in St. John's.
1957	Christopher and I are married and go to Glasgow, Scotland where Christopher enrolls in the School of Fine Arts.
1958	We return to Newfoundland where Christopher works as an engineer at Placentia Naval Base. In September we return to Glasgow.
1959	In September we both enroll at Mount Allison School of Fine Arts.
1960	I have a painting accepted in the Atlantic Awards at Dalhousie University.
1961	We graduate from Mount Allison's B.F.A. program. We both teach painting in Memorial University's Extension Department.
1962	I continue to teach and begin to paint in a corner of the dining-room.
1963	We move to Salmonier to live in the Pratt's summer cottage.
1964	I start the drawings for a book on the "Snipe" by ornithologist Les Tuck.
1967	My first solo show, at Memorial University.
1969/1971	Solo show at Morrison Gallery, Saint John, New Brunswick. Meet David Silcox, Dorothy Cameron, John Reeves. Travel to Toronto, meet Mimi Fullerton. See the work of Stella, Jim Dine.
1973	Solo show at Erindale College, University of Toronto, Erindale Campus, Mississauga. Meet David Tuck and Lyn Wynnick at this show and begin showing at "Aggregation Gallery" in Toronto. CBC's *Telescope* does a documentary "The Pratts of Newfoundland," aired nationally. "Mary Pratt: A Partial Retrospective" is shown at seven galleries in the Maritimes and Newfoundland.
1974	"The Acute Image in Canadian Art" at Owens Art Gallery, Mount Allison University.
1975	"Some Canadian Women Artists" group show at the National Gallery of Canada. "Mary Pratt: Paintings and Drawings" is shown in St. John's, Halifax, Fredericton, Vancouver, Moose Jaw, Victoria, and Banff (circulated by Memorial University Art Gallery). Work is also mentioned in *Time, Arts Canada,* and *artmagazine.*
1976	I build a studio in the garden. "Mary Pratt: A Seven-Year Survey," is my first major show at Aggregation Gallery, Toronto.
1978	Solo show "Mary Pratt: Paintings and Drawings" at Aggregation Gallery, Toronto.
1980	I go to London to visit galleries.
1981	I am represented by Mira Godard Gallery in Toronto and Calgary, and Equinox Gallery in Vancouver.
1981/82	London Regional Art Gallery, London, Ontario organizes a fourteen-year survey of my work, which circulates to nine cities in Canada. A catalogue is also published.
1983	I build a new studio in Salmonier. I agree to do paintings for a book on Canadian food written by Cynthia Wine, called *Across the Table.*
1984	I spend the summer learning water-colour techniques and I finish 144 images for *Across the Table.* John Reeves comes to photograph me in my studio and visits again in the late summer to go sailing. He teaches me quite a few tricks with the camera. We meet Joyce Zemans. We teach for a week at Banff.

1985	A show at Mira's — my first solo show with her.
1986	The Wedding Show "Aspects of a Ceremony" opens at Equinox Gallery in Vancouver.
1987	Solo show at Mira Godard's in Toronto.
1988	Part of a group show at Equinox Gallery, Vancouver.
All this work is on paper — mixed media.
1989	Show at Equinox in May.
Show at Mira Godard's in December.

◆ ———————————————

Solo Exhibitions

1967	Memorial University Art Gallery, St. John's, Newfoundland
1969-71	Morrison Gallery, Saint John, N.B.
1973	"Mary Pratt: A Partial Retrospective" travelling exhibition
1975	"Mary Pratt: Paintings and Drawings" travelling exhibition (circulated by Memorial University Art Gallery)
1976	Aggregation Gallery, Toronto
1978	Aggregation Gallery, Toronto
1981	Aggregation Gallery, Toronto
1981-82	"Mary Pratt" (a fourteen-year survey organized and circulated by the London Regional Art Gallery)
1985	Mira Godard Gallery, Toronto
1986	"Aspects of a Ceremony" Equinox Gallery, Vancouver and Mira Godard Gallery, Toronto
1989	Equinox Gallery, Vancouver
Mira Godard Gallery, Toronto

◆ ———————————————

Group Exhibitions

1961	Atlantic Awards Exhibit, Dalhousie University, Halifax, N.S.
1969-70	Canadian Graphics, National Travelling Show
1971	"Newfoundland Painters," Picture Loan Gallery, Toronto
1974	SCAN (Survey of Canadian Art Now), Vancouver Art Gallery
1974	"9 out of 10: A Survey of Contemporary Canadian Art," Art Gallery of Hamilton, Ontario; Kitchener-Waterloo Art Gallery, Ontario; the Gallery Stratford, Ontario
1974	"The Acute Image in Canadian Art," Owens Art Gallery, Mount Allison University
1975	"Towards a New Reality," Art Gallery of Ontario

1975	"Some Canadian Women Artists," National Gallery of Canada Ottawa
1976-78	"Aspects of Realism" travelling exhibition
1977	"50 Canadian Drawings," Beaverbrook Art Gallery, Fredericton, N.B.
1977	"Selecting and Collecting," Harbourfront Art Gallery, Toronto
1977-78	"Realism in Canada," Norman McKenzie Art Gallery, Regina, Saskatchewan
1979	"The Work of Art-Realism," Factory 77, Toronto
1979	"Aggregation Gallery at the Confederation Centre," Confederation Art Gallery, Charlottetown, P.E.I.
1984	"A Fish Story," Kamloops Public Art Gallery and Kamloops Museum and Archives, Kamloops, B.C.

◆ ———————————————

Principal Collections

National Gallery of Canada, Ottawa
London Regional Art Gallery, London, Ontario
The Art Gallery, Memorial University of Newfoundland
Canada Council Art Bank, Ottawa
University of Toronto, Erindale College, Mississauga, Ontario
New Brunswick Museum, Saint John, New Brunswick
University of Guelph Art Gallery, Guelph, Ontario
Beaverbrook Art Gallery, Fredericton, New Brunswick
Norcen Energy Resources, Toronto
Dofasco Inc., Hamilton, Ontario
Confederation Art Centre, Charlottetown, P.E.I.
University of New Brunswick
Canada House, London, England
C.B.C. Calgary, Alberta
Robert McLaughlin Gallery, Oshawa
Art Gallery of Nova Scotia, Halifax, Nova Scotia
C.I.L. Inc., Toronto
Acadia University, Wolfville, Nova Scotia
Canada Packers, Toronto
Owens Art Gallery, Mount Allison University, Sackville, New Brunswick
Vancouver Art Gallery, Vancouver, B.C.

◆ ─────────────────────────

Selected Bibliography

Joseph R. Smallwood, "The Book of Newfoundland," Newfoundland Book Publishers, St. John (Reproduction p. 328, 1967)

Peter Bell, "Mary Pratt: A Partial Retrospective," The Art Gallery, Memorial University of Newfoundland, St. John's, Newfoundland, June, 1973

Bill Auchtrelonie, "9 Out of 10," *artmagazine,* issue #21, Spring, 1975, p. 38-39

Harry Bruce, "The Fine Art of Familiarity," *The Canadian Magazine,* November 29, 1975

Jon Anderson, "The Emerging Group of Seven," *Time,* (Canadian Edition), Dec. 1, 1975, p. 15

Sandra Gwyn, (Excerpts from an interview), "Mary Pratt: Paintings and Drawings," The Art Gallery, Memorial University of Newfoundland, St. John's, Newfoundland, June/July, 1975

Joe Bodolai, "A Visit to Newfoundland," *artscanada,* issue 202/203 Winter, 1975-76, p. 42

Mayo Graham, "Some Canadian Women Artists," The National Gallery of Canada, Ottawa, Nov. 21 – Jan. 13, 1976, (Introduction to Catalogue, pp. 9-24 and chapter pp. 53-66)

David Burnett, "Some Canadian Women Artists," *artscanada,* issue 202/203, Winter, 75-76, p. 42

Mayo Graham, "Some Canadian Women Artists," *artmagazine,* issue #24, Dec./Jan. 1976, p. 15

Sandra Gwyn, "Mary Pratt on Mary Pratt," *artmagazine,* March, issue #25, 1976

Sandra Gwyn, "Newfoundland Renaissance," *Saturday Night,* April 1976, p. 38-45

Robert Fulford, "Mary Pratt: Paintings – A Seven Year Survey," Aggregation Gallery, Toronto, Feb. 21 – Mar. 11, 1976, (Introduction to Catalogue)

James Purdie, "Food for the Inner Man (Mind & Maw)," *The Globe & Mail,* Feb. 28, 1976

Patricia Godsell, "Enjoying Canadian Painting," General Publishing Co. Ltd., 1976, p. 236-7

Susan Hallett, "Mary Pratt, the Redeeming Realist," *Canadian Review,* May, 1976

James Purdie, "Realist takes a step toward the Surreal," *The Globe & Mail,* May 6, 1978

Joan Murray, "Mary Pratt," *artscanada,* (review), May, 1978

Gary Michael Dault, "I like Paint Better than Realism," *Toronto Star,* May 6, 1978, "A Joy of Surfaces," *Saturday Night,* September, 1978, (Cover & p. 8)

Stephen Kimber, "Mary Pratt, Artist," *Atlantic Insight,* Sept. 1979, (Cover and Article p. 24-26)

Joan Murray, "Joan Murray talking with Mary Pratt," *Arts Atlantic,* Spring, 1979, p. 38-41

Susan MacKay, "Women Artists in Canada," *Atlantus,* Autumn, 1979

Joan Murray, "Some Contemporary Women Artists in Canada," *Fireweed,* Summer, 1979

Samuel Stevens, "Treasures of Canada," editor Alinander Scala, 1980, p. 63, (Reproduction)

Jerrold Morris, *100 Years of Canadian Drawings,* Methuen Press, 1980, p. 169

John Bentley Mays, "Twelve (Women) Artists Just Grind Non-Art Axes," *The Globe and Mail,* March 8, 1980, p. 11

London Regional Art Gallery, "Mary Pratt," Exhibition Catalogue, 1981

Harry Thurston, "Christopher and Mary: the first couple of Contemporary Canadian Art," *Equinox,* March/April 1982, pp. 72-83

Anne Collins, "Mary Pratt: In and Out of the Kitchen," *City Woman,* Summer, 1982, pp. 54-62

Morgan Annan, "Mary and Christopher Pratt," *Newfoundland Lifestyle,* Fall, 1984, pp. 24-27

Cynthia Wine, Watercolours by Mary Pratt, *Across the Table,* Prentice-Hall, Toronto, 1985

Ellen Fee, "Mary Pratt: Equinox Gallery Vancouver," *Vanguard,* February, 1987, pp. 38-39

Christopher Hume, "Mary Pratt — Turning on to Everyday Objects," *Art Impressions,* Summer, 1988, pp. 20-22

Patricia Molloy, "Mary Pratt: Recent Paintings," *Arts Atlantic,* Spring/Summer, 1988, p. 21

◆ ─────────────────────────

Photos facing page 1, from left to right:

Top: Mary on her tricycle, Waterloo Row, Fredericton (1940); Mary and her father, W.J. West, Fredericton (1946); Mary West one-half hour before becoming Mary Pratt (1957 — Harvey Studio). *Middle:* Mary Margaret Coburn, Mary's maternal great-grandmother; Mary as a flower girl at the marriage of her cousin, Polly Brown. *Bottom:* The late King George VI, and Queen Elizabeth, now the Queen Mother; Christopher Pratt (1988 — Barbara Wangersky); Mary and Christopher at Mount Allison (1955); With Barby, Anne, Baby Ned and John (1964); Christopher with Anne (left) and Barby (right) in Salmonier.

Photos facing page 23, from left to right:

Top: Oil painting, 1960, "Yellow Apples on a White Cloth," one of Mary's works as a student; "Oil Stove" by Christopher (for which Mary posed). *Middle:* Mary in her studio (John Reeves). *Bottom:* Photography for "Herring on a Salt Bag"; Mary's studio (John Reeves).

◆